THE D

100 days and lessons in corporate communications

Dedicated to:

Ben, Charlie and Jamie.

"Those friends thou hast, and their adoption tried,
Grapple them unto thy soul with hoops of steel."

Polonius to Laertes: *Hamlet* 1, iii

"To set a gloss on faint deeds, hollow welcomes,
Recanting goodness, sorry ere 'tis shown;
But where there is true friendship, there
needs none."

Timon: *Timon of Athens* 1, ii

"I went out to Charing Cross to see Major General Harrison hanged, drawn and quartered; which was done there, he looking as cheerful as any man could in that condition."

Samuel Pepys, diarist (1633–1703)

I FIRST MET Arthur Shilling during his second year at our university. He was studying Shakespeare and I was teaching an option on *Romeo and Juliet*. I found him to be an attentive student and he was most keen to take part in the Dotheby Players' productions, a motley crew of literature students who had a decent stab at a couple of Shakespeare productions each year, led by yours truly. I discovered that Arthur was particularly keen on Shakespearian stagecraft and was more than adept at holding his own with Mercutio.

He began to apply for a number of jobs in his final year and eventually secured a position as a corporate communications executive with Grammond Hopes, an international bank with over 100,000 people around the world on its payroll. The 2009 financial crisis seemed to have left the behemoth unscathed, which must say something for its management.

Arthur was very keen to keep an email diary of his first year with GH (as he grew to call his corporate parents) and I agreed that I would advise where I could on aspects of communication that he found difficult. I can't say that I am *the* expert on such matters and certainly modesty should prevail but, between my first attempt at academia and this current bout of bliss, I was, for over five years, head of corporate communications at Franklin,

Cakes and Dribs Financial Services in London. I have also written a number of articles on the subject of good communication, particularly in times of financial downturn. Arthur thought me something of a communications expert – flattering certainly, although I did point out that not all the new gizmos and widgets of social networking were, or indeed are, always 100% familiar to me.

Once young Arthur had finished his first year or so with Gammond Hopes and had taken the consequences of his successes and failures, I'm ashamed to say that I decided to publish his email diary to add a few modest coppers to my lean pension fund. Arthur protested, of course, maintaining that I had made money from his experiences, although I did point out that this was exactly what any author or playwright does one way or another. Didn't Shakespeare? And anyway, I remarked to the young fellow – smarting as he was in a rather undignified way – that there were lessons to be learnt and, since I had provided many of said lessons, then surely I had a right to some of the gain?

He didn't necessarily agree and threatened all kinds of ripostes and actions, none of which came to much apart from a few solicitors' letters and I do like to think that we're still the best of friends. Anyway, here you are – the learnings according to me about the travail of one Arthur Shilling BA (most richly deserved, even if his Fool in *King Lear* was oddly similar to The Joker from the *Batman* film franchise).

Professor S Charteris
Still Waters, Bridgetown, Barbados

Chapter One

"Confusion now hath made his masterpiece!"

Macduff: *Macbeth* (Act II, iii)

1

From: Arthur Shilling [arthur.shilling@gammondhopes.com]
Sent: 04/18/2011 8.16 AM GMT
To: Steven Charteris [stevencharteris@staracademy.com]
Subject: To begin at the beginning

Steven

You did say that I might call you by your first name, so I really hope that you don't mind. I can revert very quickly to Professor Charteris, if you wish. By the way, I've just watched the black and white film *The Browning Version*. You know, Terence Rattigan and starring Michael Redgrave. Have you seen it? Extremely good and the oratory at the end can't be matched. Reminded me a bit of you actually. No offence.

Well, I arrived at the head office of Grammond Hopes Bank half an hour early. Wanted to create a good impression. Was asked to sign a special book at reception – I hadn't brought any of my joining papers with me. Bit daft really, because I *had* been reminded. I also had to ask Mr Alan Trebbish (that's what it said on the receptionist's badge) if I could borrow his pen. That was a moment of great anxiety for him, because it was a Mont Blanc Starwalker Resin Line, and the process caused me no little embarrassment because the book was on a short metal lead and I had to clamber onto the reception desk in order to put pen to paper. Alan told me to get down.

Anyway, that done and with my badge cheerily clipped onto my jacket lapel, I made my way up to the 7th floor in what is called the slow lift (one that stops at every floor automatically whether you want it to or not). By the time we reached (what I now know as) my floor, the lift was empty and, for some reason, I was humming *Yellow Submarine* to myself.

Outside the lift there stood a very tall, gaunt and severe-looking Indian gentleman, probably in his late thirties, who introduced himself to me as Mr Bose. "Hello, Mr Both," I said. He corrected me with a curt, "It's Bose, not Boat." I believe that this was the point at which our relationship momentarily broke down.

Mr Bose (née Both or Boat) took me through three sets of glass security doors and then we walked past about a hundred metres of filing cabinets. He ran a long thumbnail along the ridges of the cabinet doors, making a kind of Pink Floyd staccato beat. "That's very good," I said. He just turned round, gave me a bit of a stare and said nothing.

"This is where you sit," said Mr Bose, gesturing at a long glass-topped desk on which sat a laptop docking pod and a brand new Sony laptop. Also on the desk was an empty, but sparkling, set of see-through plastic pen and pencil holders and a few envelopes with my name typed on each. And there was a white phone along with a box containing the very latest BlackBerry Bold.

"Wait here, please Mr Penny. Mrs Sourdough will be joining you in a moment to begin your induction. You will also meet Mr Rattles, Head of EMEA Communications, and Jez Staffordshire. Mr Staffordshire is Director, Comms IPIDL."

I confess to nearly laughing out loud because I was sure he'd said "I piddle". Anyway, of course I didn't and he hadn't really, but Mr Bose just wandered off again, making the filing cabinets his very own drum kit. I was not a little miffed that he'd managed a tit for tat re surnames. Game on, I thought.

The day passed quickly as indeed did much of the week. I duly met Mr Derek Rattles, Head of EMEA Communications, who stared out of his 34th floor corner office window most of the time we talked. "The view on the 41th floor is astonishing of course, particularly from the boardroom. The table there seats 56 and is made from one piece of Javanese wood. The Chairman commissioned it." He was concerned as to my speechwriting capabilities because it seems that the Chairman's scriptwriter is in hospital and the Communications Department is responsible for filling the gap. Executives at GH make lots of speeches and apparently I shall be penning some of those. I also have to help with the delivery of a number of corporate events. Not sure yet what that entails, but it sounds exciting and very rock and roll. And, there's an amateur dramatics group here called the Shakedown Players and they put on a Shakespeare every few months. I'm going to audition for something I think. I have great affection for my Dotheby Players days – under your tutelage of course.

Once I got used to my laptop, a latest Vaio (which I'm to take with me everywhere), I started to find out all I needed to know about the company's culture and procedures. The staff restaurant is great by the way and you can get any kind of sandwich filling imaginable, although a very pretty girl called Zalautha Derong, who sits at the end of my row of desks, tends to eat a family bag of cheese and onion crisps in one sitting along with two cheese and chutney sandwiches. Every day. She's from Côte d'Ivoire apparently and they don't have much in the way of cheese and chutney combinations in what were once the French colonies. Her English is poor and I don't quite know why she's in communications or indeed what she actually does.

On Tuesday I was copied in on the following emails – by mistake I think:

From: Jez Staffordhire [jez.staffordhire@gammondhopes.com]
Sent: 04/13/2011 09:35 PM CET
To: Khalif ALMOUN
Subject: Communications Executive Mainstream UK

Khalif hey. Hope all's well and that the rash is much better. Just a quick heads-up to let you know that an Arthur Shilling is joining the Comms mob. I assume that you've seen the paperwork on him, so you'll know a little of his background. He's a newbie and this is his first job. Now that he's one of your direct or dotted line reports, can you please ensure that he takes on old Bathopsope's caseload? Is Batho still in hospital by the way? Oh yes, and I think that the new boy should get stuck into the Chairman's speeches now that Brian Keys left under such unfortunate circumstances. Did we ever get the real story one wonders? And is *he* out of hospital yet? Thanks in advance and I'll see you in a couple of weeks.

Sent from Jez Staffordshire's iPhone

From: Khalif Almoun [khalif.almoun@gammondhopes.com]
Sent: 04/17/2011 20:37 PM CET
To: Barbara Sourdough
Bcc: Arthur Shilling
Subject: Art Shilling: Communications Executive
Mainstream UK

Hi B

Thing is the new guys strting on Tues and Im not bk in UK til
Weds so cn you hlp out and make sure that he gets the ususal?
We need to put him to wrk on the spech stff for Flattergleich's
speeches. Theres other stuff but thatl do for strtrs.

Need anythung AMERICUN?!

K

Khalf Almoun
Tri-State Corporate Business | Gammond Hopes North America
4520 5th Avenue NYC
New York 10398
Phone (1) 282 567 2999
Mob (1) 689 987 99021

2

From: Arthur Shilling [arthur.shilling@gammondhopes.com]
Sent: 04/20/2011 20.16 PM GMT
To: Steven Charteris [stevencharteris@staracademy.com]
Subject: Getting stuck in

Steven (are you *sure* you don't mind?)

I wasn't overly impressed with that little email flurry and I haven't met Mr Almoun yet, even though I'm told he's not 'Stateside' anymore.

I have now been introduced to a vast number of managers and senior executives, each of whom has smiled tautly and shaken my hand with varying levels of dampness. One fellow's hand was almost liquid. But hey, when you're minor royalty this is what you have to do! Shake hands. Meet the people. Kiss babies.

The introductions did seem endless as did assurances that I was going to light up the Communications Department. Questions came fast: by the by did I know thingy who was also at Durham studying Microbiology and wasn't doodah's son, daughter, nephew, niece at Durham too and did I perhaps know Deidre Numskull? But the really odd thing was the language these people spoke. I was surrounded by the echoes of: "Ah yes, well the AER has hit the AIM with a bang, but nothing's dissolved yet and the share of wallet is clear blue. And, my oh my, the CDO and CGT are getting a walloping across the pond going forward. Did you get the notes on the GEB? Did the cookies get cut? Oh good and did Mike show you what he'd managed to deliver in terms of his TER thinking? Bob shared that view did he?" And so on. Well I suppose I'll get used to it.

Mr Bose sits near me and continues to be a bit weird; he rarely smiles even when the office jokes are very funny indeed. However, I must say that if he sees that I'm having a problem with something he's there like Jeeves and always spends time ensuring that everything's clear. If people, actually anyone no matter how senior, asks me a question to which I have no answer, my Mr Bose will gently but firmly help me out. I have noticed that he has occasional very quiet phone calls where he speaks earnestly into his mobile. He's totally absorbed in the conversation with whoever it is. To the point that he leans so far back in his Herman Miller Sayl chair (with suspension back) that I fear for his safety.

By the way, *my* seating accommodation is even better than Mr Bose's. I have a very grand Herman Miller Aeron chair. *All* the chairs are Herman Miller – all black, but a variety of models. I ought to buy a few Herman Miller shares I think.

Arthur

3

From: Arthur Shilling [arthur.shilling@gammondhopes.com]
Sent: 04/28/2011 19.16 PM GMT
To: Steven Charteris [stevencharteris@staracademy.com]
Subject: Inducted

Steven (do please say if this is embarrassing – I'm quite comfortable with Prof Charteris)

Well, the first couple of weeks have blown past in a bit of a grey whirlwind. I've been well and truly inducted (or perhaps, more painfully, induced) and my feet haven't really touched the ground.

I'm not complaining even though I don't get home until after 9 each evening.

We're supposed to be running something of a paperless office here, although there are reams of photocopied and printed stuff all over the place. And people just rip open new packs of paper, take a few sheets out and chuck the remaining sheets wherever. There needs to be a green campaign. Or one on sustainability.

I'm told that I will indeed be embarking on speech-writing next week. Can't wait. I cracked my knuckles in order to start being creative but just succeeded in really hurting a tendon. I'm also going to begin some serious report writing too and I have to start thinking about event management. I must ask someone, discreetly of course, what EMEA means. Acronyms are us!

One thing I have discovered is how to be an automatic expert on anything. They all do it here. Look at the columns below. You just choose one word from each column and, hey presto, you're an expert. I haven't dared use it yet, but I will:

Column 1	Column 2	Column 3
Integrated	management	options
Overall	organisational	flexibility
Systematised	monitored	capability
Parallel	reciprocal	mobility
Functional	digital	programming
Responsive	logistical	concept

Optimal	transitional	time-phase
Synchronised	incremental	projection
Compatible	third generation	hardware
Balanced	policy	contingency

I did say "Balanced organisational programming, anyone?" to Mr Bose, but he didn't smile, although two people in the next desk section stuck their thumbs up. I think that they were impressed. Mrs Sourdough says that my induction will be completed once I've met Khalif Almoun and the Chairman. I quite like Mrs Sourdough. (Her first name's Angelina and her second Barbara, but the poor thing doesn't look like an Angelina as in Jolie.) There is no Mr Sourdough and I feel a bit sorry for her. She's very efficient, but insists on leaving Post-its all over the place that I can never properly decipher – and which, in turn, cause a great amount of tutting.

4

From: Arthur Shilling [arthur.shilling@gammondhopes.com]
Sent: 05/4/2011 19.16 PM GMT
To: Steven Charteris [stevencharteris@staracademy.com]
Subject: I'm a speechwriter!

Steven, hope all's well with you and yours.

I understand from the grapevine that Mrs Charteris won her examination board tribunal case. Bravo her. What happened to the orthodox Jewish person then? Did he get his fur hat back?

Guess what? I've been given my first brief to write a speech, not for the Chairman – whom I've still not yet met – but for the group head of Internal Communications, Mr Flattergleich. English isn't his mother tongue, but he does speak a wide variety of languages. The subject of the speech is 'Moral Turpitude in a Balanced Marketplace'. Yes, I know. It's for an industry after-dinner slot and has to be around 30 minutes' worth of pure delight. I thought I'd start of with a Chekovian quote about fear and dishonesty. And then maybe a financial services joke. Mr Bose says that I need to hit the ground running with this one.

I've already seen Mr Flattergleich, or Hermann as his close colleagues call him, at the podium and he is not the best speech-maker in the world. He grips the lectern for dear life and, when he moves away, he jams his hands in his pockets and the waistband of his trousers moves downwards dangerously close to what might be termed indecent if he was a woman. I wonder whether I'm allowed to give him some polite theatrical tips? Better not. He does forever jingle the change in his pockets which makes him look somewhat as if he is exploring his testicular regions, but I can't tell him to stop that. At the time I saw him make a presentation, three girls at the back of the auditorium were giggling. The lights were full on and nobody could read the PowerPoint – the font was tiny and the whole thing could have been double Dutch, or German. Probably was. Mr Bose says that Mr F continues to confirm his status as the world's worst corporate communicator. I hope that he doesn't say that too loud.

Mr F currently has a complete lack of awareness of, or willingness to acknowledge, the need to communicate well and appropriately with the media and public. It's to be my role to help him a) be aware and b) do something about it. I do like him and I think that we can work together well. I recall Prof Waddington saying that it's the job of a leader (Julius Caesar I think he used as an example) to inspire belief and confidence so that people are moved to follow the direction they set. The ability to lead and inspire is particularly important in these tough times, said Prof Wad, when people from all industries and sectors are feeling pressured, fearful and embattled. Except, of course, when they get metaphorically stabbed. Mind you, Jez Staffordshire (Director Comms IPIDL) is no better. Jez's hectoring tone onstage is exacerbated by a rhythmic, banging fist gesture that becomes quite repetitive and the structure of his speech is often laden with clichéd pairs, contrasts and repetitions that are delivered with a cadence that lacks sufficient modulation. That's actually what Mr Bose said. Privately of course and I wasn't supposed to hear.

Arthur

5

From: Arthur Shilling [arthur.shilling@gammondhopes.com]
Sent: 05/20/2011 04.16 AM GMT
To: Steven Charteris [stevencharteris@staracademy.com]
Subject: I might be the new Jon Favreau!

Steven

I hope all's well with you. Mr Bose told me that creating phrases using that list of words in the three column buzz generator that I sent you is stupid at best and damaging to communications at worst. I was a bit miffed, but then I actually think he's right.

I went for my first Shakedown Players audition last week. They're doing *Hamlet* and said they needed a decent Fortinbras, but I confess that I was hoping for something in the higher echelons of the play. Yes, I know – no such thing as a small part. But you did agree that my Mercutio was something else, even if you did think my Fool from *King Lear* was slightly excitable. I didn't read for the lead in *Hamlet*, although the chap who did has a lisp. Doesn't sound right to me, particularly if he can only say 'quethtion'. Pretty fundamental, I'd have thought. There are second round auditions this weekend.

Have met the Chairman now but, alas, still not the elusive Mr Khalif Almoun. People still say he's around and about, but obviously sees his care in the community (i.e. me) unnecessary.

To get into the Chairman's office you have to go through umpteen different security checks and rooms with secretaries and smart people (who don't look much older than me) called PAs. I asked Mr Bose how you become a PA (something very executive and very important apparently), but he just ignored the question.

At the meeting, there were people I hadn't met before – nearly all with white hair and crisp white shirts under expensive suits in dark blue or bold and charcoal grey stripes. Also in attendance was Derek Rattles, Head of EMEA Comms and Jez Staffordshire, Communications Director of IPIDL which, lest you smirk, stands for Integrated Performance and International Development Link. If you think that's good, we have INKT, PUPS, THIES, DOODUL, PRAK, ARK, EEK, CAP, CIP, CARP, CRAP (I kid you not) and STOOL. The last two have of course become the office running joke.

The Chairman listened to the briefing session for the Forum that he's hosting. It's all about the future and how the bank will be prepared (or not) to manage in the 2030s. Mind you, the majority of these sharp-suited gents won't be around then or will be drooling gently as they snooze in front of the cricket in The Happy Days Home for Gentlefolk. But the notion of the Forum is strong – looking at how corporate leaders can use what information we have now for future planning. What's really interesting is that the programme for the event will include top experts from all walks of life: sustainability, climate change, water shortage, microfinance, world security, law and order, terrorism, causes of conflict, migration, world demography and so on. The Chairman has apparently long thought that his direct reports and senior management team are too restricted in their thinking. He wants more 'what if' scenarios out in the open. I'm to write the first draft of his opening address. I blushed prettily when my name was mentioned.

During the meeting he looked at me only once when we were introduced. I was ready to stick out my hand to shake his, but he wasn't up for that. He just had this gimlet stare, nodded and then spent much of the meeting looking at the mid-distance, which is apparently the offing and used by sailors in days of yore.

There was a woman in the meeting (Dephne Hong and no, I haven't spelt her first name incorrectly, and it's pronounced Deaf Knee) who's in charge of events or, at any rate, senior executives' events. She organises everything and gets the production companies involved plus all the PowerPoint, guest speakers and so on. She's from Hong Kong and very bossy – not that the two are mutually exclusive of course. She also has a really annoying habit of finishing her sentences when you're not expecting them to be finished. But it's her bossiness that stands out. Even when the Chairman commented on some aspect that didn't fit with her well laid out plans, she would say "Well, Chairman. We wouldn't want. We wouldn't want to do that. Because to do that…" I thought that the Chairman would snap back that he could do what he bloody well pleased, but he didn't and neither did he tell. Her. To Bugger. Off. He just gave her the steely-eyed look and then nodded and asked for better particulars.

There were refreshments on the table – coffee, tea, expensive continental biscuits (I was desperate to have one of those, but didn't dare) – but the only people making use of these supplies was the Chairman himself and IPDL's finest, Mr Staffordshire, who had a slight tremble of the hand as he poured some coffee, only managing to deposit a little on the beautiful, burnished table top.

Mr Staffordshire (I still can't call him Jez and neither does he encourage the familiarity) came out with odd comments when asked about his view on aspects of the Chairman's Forum. Things, if memory serves, like: "Communication hin the workplace, Chairman, his one of the keys to hay successful company. Hemployees need to be haware of the company vision and hear from leadership that they matter to the bottom line. That's the happroach to take I think." Everyone looked at him in wild surmise and Miss Dephne Hong filled in the ensuing gap with some titbit about the Forum's organisation. Initially, there are to be three events dotted around the world – Dubai, New York and possibly London. Maybe I'll be invited to go, although I suspect that the white-haired mob in the room plus various acolytes all expect the same thing.

Nobody brought up the topic of the Chairman's address until the very end of the meeting when Mr Staffordshire casually invited me to discuss content. I sat bolt upright, spilling Dephne's juice, with absolutely no clue as to what the content should be or what I was supposed to say. My face burnt red and sweat trickled down my back. The room spun (span? spanned? spurned?) and my vision blurred. Nobody had said that this might happen. Everyone was staring at me and the Chairman was fiddling with his coffee cup. I froze and then Mr Staffordshire said something like, "Hunfortunately, today's hemployee orften feels that he, or indeed she, is not 'eard and does not 'ave open lines of communication wiv, ah, management. We should hattempt to over-communicate rather than under — as knowledgeable hemployees lead to higher productivity and job satisfaction. Plus. Plus. Perhaps that should be the start point?" Well, of course that didn't help and the situation was only saved by Mr Rattles saying that I would deliver an outline of speech content by this time tomorrow.

6

From: Arthur Shilling [arthur.shilling@gammondhopes.com]
Sent: 06/25/2011 18.16 PM GMT
To: Steven Charteris [stevencharteris@staracademy.com]
Subject: The plot thickens

Dear Steven

I got the part of Horatio! Yes. Not bad for a first attempt I think you might agree. The guy with the lisp did get Hamlet and everyone seems to think that he's an extraordinary actor. I can't see it myself. He's about my age and went to some drama school or other. Not a very appetising Hamlet I have to say – spots all over the place and seriously on the chubby side. I can't really believe that this chap will present some of the greatest language and philosophies the world has ever known with the appropriate conviction. We'll see. There's a very fit person playing Ophelia and we've chatted a bit. She works for the GH Private Bank and is in fancy offices over towards St James'.

Well, I've started the précis for the Chairman's Forum opening address/speech. I was given a briefing document by Deaf Knee and spent all night on background research. The speech is running to about eighteen pages of bullet points. Mr Bose said that this was too long and that the basic tenets should fit on one page, tops. He said that he'd show me what he meant later. Hmm. He might have a point although my outline *is* thorough. I have had to cut and paste stuff from Google which makes the style a bit awkward, but anyone reading it will get the idea. Mr Bose says that just cutting and pasting from the Internet is a facile idea and will teach me little. The key, he says, is understanding and that communication is about two things: understanding and explaining. I shall submit the précis tomorrow. Reduced a little. I was thinking sixteen pages. Various people want to see it. Yikes.

We have a monthly departmental meeting with all staff members. If someone can't attend then they have to dial in and some staff from overseas are in the room via video conferencing. The aim of the meeting is a bit vague, but we all have a laugh. We get updates on the company's business, departmental matters, major staffing updates (me on this occasion) and stuff about new policies. Everyone's invited to ask questions or make considered contributions. Few of us seem to do that. Neither the asking or the considering. Sometimes we're given praise and teams are told that they're doing a good job – contribution to the success and morale of the company, department or, as Mrs Sourdough keeps saying, "some such thing".

I was asked to present myself to the meeting. I was prepared for that. After I started, I said, "Can you hear me at the back?" Nobody laughed. Then I said, "It's OK, I'm here all week." Again, nobody laughed. Mind you, Jenny Barstiff (another newbie) spent 50% of her speech with her head down looking at the floor and her shoulders were shaking. Someone muttered that perhaps she'd got new shoelaces and was examining them for quality control.

Then Mr Rattles spoke. This would be a treat I thought. No, this was not a treat. We had data-heavy slides on GDP, output, employment, house prices, inter-bank lending rates, debt levels, liquidity, equity prices, exchange rates… and on and on. I was reminded of that great line or two from *Henry IV* Part II (Act 3, scene i):

> "O sleep! O gentle sleep!
> Nature's soft nurse, how have I frighted thee,
> That thou no more wilt weigh my eyelids down
> And steep my senses in forgetfulness?"

Mr Rattles' message was essentially that in GH EMEA Communications' – i.e. his – view (note to self, must find out what EMEA means), things were improving… slightly. He thinks that over the next three years, growth could be anything from -2% to +5% (nothing like hedging your bets… a bit like saying rain is possible in an English weather forecast!).

Were all those slides really necessary? Especially given a mixed bunch of attendees, only a small proportion of whom understood finance? Surely the message about a slight recovery could have been conveyed in a more engaging way that didn't involve bombarding us with graphs. Perhaps he could have picked the top ten indicators and talked a little about each of them? In my mind this data dump of a speech was made worse by the stark contrast with the next speaker. Jeff Goodenhardt was something in the US communications team and simply a brilliant presenter. He spoke for a good 25 minutes without a PowerPoint slide in sight. I did think though that his attitude towards Mr Flattergleich was a touch contemptuous. Mr F is, after all, the grand *fromage*. It is said among the corridors of power (or the water coolers) that Mr Goodenhardt doesn't much care for Germans and wants the Group Head of Communications title for himself. Hmm.

Best

Arthur

7

From: Arthur Shilling [arthur.shilling@gammondhopes.com]
Sent: 07/07/2011 21.16 PM GMT
To: Steven Charteris [stevencharteris@staracademy.com]
Subject: Hard work

Steven

Well, my basic speech outline for the Chairman's introductory remarks re the first Chairman's Worldwide Integrated Strategic Enterprise (WISE) Executive Forum was a total disaster. Too long. Mr Bose was quite right. It should have been short and sharp. He was very kind and reshaped it for me. When I showed it to Mr Rattles again, he just looked at me and nodded slowly. I think that's a good sign, compounded by the fact that Jenny Barstiff, the other newbie with whom I'm reasonably good mates, rushed round to my desk, put her beautiful face close to mine and breathed a huge "You did good, bub!" at me, then twirled like a ballerina and zoomed off. Mr Bose looked over and I swear I saw him smile faintly or perhaps it was just a twitch of the mouth. Or indigestion. Or, as Mrs Sourdough said *en passant*, "some such thing".

I've been spending time with the bossy Deaf Knee and I now know all the organisational and production details plus the content relating to the forthcoming Executive Forum. She said, "Next time. Next time we will meet the production company. And you. You will come with me." So I'm looking forward to that. Whatever it means.

I did some decent research with Mr Bose's help. The event will, amongst other things, cover the future of careers and the question: 'If I were staring my career all over again, where would I start it?' We're getting a futurist to speak – not somebody who reads one's palm, but someone who studies the future and makes predictions about it based on current trends. Then we're going to look at what Dephne Hong calls wildcards and their potential impact on the future of financial services. Demography's a big thing in this and we've got a research director from the Institute of Migration Studies based in New York. Demography and its influence on the world economy in 2030 is apparently big on the Chairman's agenda. We've also lined up a professor from Oxford's Department of Zoology to speak about the human effects of a changed world by 2030. Not quite sure where we're going with that one.

'Who will rule the world in 2030?' is another of the questions on which the Chairman's keen to get something of an answer. We're trying to get someone to speak about the Middle East and its political prospects. Deaf Knee Hong seemed to think that this task might fall to me. Not to talk about the subject of course (haha), but to find someone who could. Ms Hong has someone in mind to speak about Latin America and its ability to sustain long-term growth. That's as far as we've got and that's only the People part of the event. The other three sections are Politics, Behaviour and Business. I think Ms Hong likes me and finds me a kindred spirit. Although, when I left the meeting, she almost crushed my hand in her office door in her rush to get me out.

I've had two *Hamlet* rehearsals so far. Because I'm in the opening scene, I tried very hard to show the assembled company that I was a seasoned player who understood the Shakespearian text and its depth of meaning. Trouble was, next door the company's restaurant staff were sharing ribald jokes and my words were lost amidst clanking crockery being trundled about on trolleys or shrieks of adenoidal laughter. Still, early days. I remain doubtful about the chap with the lisp playing the troubled Dane. Why on earth would anyone consider that Hamlet had a lisp or any speech defect? Where's the proof? I know, of course, that we're all meant to love our brethren come what may. But I confess that I don't.

Best

Arthur

8

From: Arthur Shilling [arthur.shilling@gammondhopes.com]
Sent: 07/20/2011 11.16 PM GMT
To: Steven Charteris [stevencharteris@staracademy.com]
Subject: Busy

Steven

Not much in this report. Tremendously busy preparing for the Chairman's WISE Executive Forum. Mr Rattles is very pleased with progress. Met production company in trendy West London offices. Lots of leather-bound notebooks, jeans and T-shirts with slogans like 'Mash It Up', 'Superman Was So Wrong', 'Armageddon' or 'The Isle of Wight Rules' writ large on the fronts or backs. One had 'Led Zeppelin Still Rocks', which my father might have worn back in the early 70s. There followed a small debate as to whether it should be 'rock' or 'rocks'. Of course, *we* both know which is correct.

Our producer on this event is a woman called Raspberry Jenkins – honestly! She's pretty, pert, capable and uses jargon that I just don't get. She also speaks very loudly even if one is but a metre from her pretty head. She is respected or, more likely, feared. But, early days.

Ms Hong is treated like a deity and I had to listen again to her story about some incident when she was nightclubbing in Hong Kong. You'd think that she'd change the story or joke. I have to fix a rictus grin every time she gets to the punchline. The agency folk fall about as if Ms Hong has said the funniest thing ever. During the meeting, people kept joining us, each saying how sorry he or she was for being so dreadfully late. Then they'd spend a good few minutes arranging notebooks and other mysteriously wondrous stationery on the table, pour water and generally make sure everyone knew that they had arrived. Apparently, I have to chair the next meeting at head office because Ms Hong is abroad. Double yikes.

By the by, in connection with the WISE Forum, we might invite you to speak about 'whither literature of the future'. How would you feel about that? The fee's not bad although, of course, I'd need to negotiate that with you! Must rush and exit pursued by the veritable bear.

I wonder if I have some Danish blood in me from somewhere. I think that one of my ancestors had the name Holstein. Another was called Harald Klak. Yet another was called Gyrd or Gnuppa, so that might signify something.

Arthur (or, quite possibly, Olaf)

9

From: Arthur Shilling [arthur.shilling@gammondhopes.com]
Sent: 07/26/2011 19.16 PM GMT
To: Steven Charteris [stevencharteris@staracademy.com]
Subject: Busy, busy, busy

Dear Steven

Mr Bose has seemed very much below par of late, although he always has time to help me if I get stuck on anything. He's extraordinarily patient. I wondered if he was a bit off-hand with me, but apparently that's just the way he is. You can tell though that the top brass think he's brill just by the way they ask for his advice and defer to his views. I wonder why he's not been promoted to a higher grade. *My* grade, by the way, is F19. Don't even ask.

I've just met the elusive Khalif Almoun, my direct boss! He dashed into the lift having stopped the doors from closing – something which everyone thought was terribly funny as indeed did he. I thought it was stupid and dangerous. Anyway, he looked round the lift and his eye caught my security badge and therefore my name. "Arty! Arty!" he shouted, elbowing a large lady out of the way who didn't seem to mind in the least. "At last!" he yelled. And he then proceeded to give me a huge hug in the process of which he drove his loins embarrassingly close into mine. I'm sure everyone made one and one add up to three. Anyway, he told me that he had his eye on me and that he'd heard good things. He got out of the lift before I did and, as the doors closed, gave me a big wink. Everyone in the lift fell silent and looked at me.

Arty

10

From: Arty Shilling [arthur.shilling@gammondhopes.com]
Sent: 07/29/2011 07.16 AM GMT
To: Steven Charteris [stevencharteris@staracademy.com]
Subject: Mr Bose

Steven

A short missive this. The Forum plans are moving on apace and I've just been told to manage a tweet campaign to major clients.

Social media's the thing apparently. Mugged up on Twitter and discovered from Mrs Sourdough that it's actually quite straightforward. Very similar to how I use it myself. Do you have a Twitter account? Facebook?

Mr Almoun, now often seen rushing around in lifts and going to meetings, but never seemingly able to arrive, has taken to winking at me on a regular basis and is always pointing a forefinger at me and then clicking his fingers as if shooting a finger gun. He seems to like me and smiles a great deal. Nobody knows what he does or where he goes.

I have to send tweets to a number of the bank's clients alerting them to some special deals. The marketing department has penned the limited words (140 characters max) that I'm to send and I have the contact lists. I have no idea what the offer means or who the recipients are. Not my job to know I suppose. And, before you ask, the person who's supposed to be doing this is ill. The series of messages were to link certain discounts and special deals to various hashtags, which would have been fine if the hashtags hadn't been completely unrelated. "What's a hashtag?" I hear you mutter as you butter a small crumpet that I suspect you still take with afternoon tea. They're short messages on services such as Twitter and Facebook. The tag can include one or more words or phrases prefixed with a hash symbol (#), with multiple words linked, like those in: "#Shakespeare is my favourite kind of #playwright." Then, a person can search for the string #Shakespeare and this tagged word will appear in the search engine results. It's a device usually used for consumable products. OK?

Anyway, I did all that I was told so to do and sent everything out only to find that what had gone out was my tweet to my new best friend in *Hamlet*, Graham Graveling. He's playing Claudius and is outstanding. Totally gets it. Although in the scene where he's saying his prayers and our lisping thethp debateth whether to chop hith unnklth head off there and then – well Grahamth actually *really* praying to thumwun about thumthing and it'th very dithturbing. Anyway my message to him was "The lithper wath a hoot – fiddling with hith zipth in the change between Actth III and IV, he caught his thingy!" Innocent enough of course. However that's what went to some 6,000 folk in the financial community last Thursday. Whoops is an understatement. But thank the very heavens that I wrote 'thingy' and not something more colloquial!

This egregious example of hashtag spamming occurred when I further tweeted: "#GammondHope – join the database and receive a £1,000 gift card". Well, obviously someone had rewritten the real message and thought that the company offering 6,000 people a £1,000 gift was very funny. In response to the obvious scandal, the marketing department quickly removed the tweets and apologised repeatedly to all recipients and relevant clients, few of whom were even slightly amused. Gloria Mishmash (I think her name is) of the PR department said to me that I was very, very stupid. And then she slammed the phone down. Khalif Almoun came up to my desk (unheard of) and sat on its edge after having carefully moved an apple core. "It's this traditional approach from which big businesses need to move away," he said sadly. There was not a sniff of a wink or the shooting finger. He said instead, "Well, we must show that we understand how our social media actions affect others and you have to be willing to follow up. By the way, you might get fired." And then he bounced off clapping Mr Bose on the shoulder and singing *Hey Jude* very loudly.

Professor, I do believe that I'm in trouble. I also believe that I have no Danish blood in my veins.

Arty

>

From: Steven Charteris [stevencharteris@staracademy.com]
Sent: 08/02/2011 09.16 AM GMT
To: Arthur Shilling [arthur.shilling@gammondhopes.com]
Subject: Your first weeks in your new job

Dear Arthur

I will carry on with Arthur if that's OK with you. Arty doesn't really work for me. Danish derivatives don't hold much adventure so I'm glad that you dismissed that angle of your possible ancestry. I'm delighted that you are more comfortable with your origins. Thanks for asking after Mrs C, who doesn't quite remember you, but was grateful nonetheless for your concern.

Well, well. You have indeed started off with something of a bang. Don't finish with a bang or indeed an Eliot whimper come to that. Anyway, congratulations on a lively beginning. Some observations if I may:

Arrival
- Arthur, you really should have read your joining instructions. That would have helped you settle in better and arrive with an understanding of what was expected. And you ought to carry a pen always!

- If you meet someone for the first time, make it a priority to understand the pronunciation of his or her name before saying it.

- Be careful that your extra-mural activities don't take too much of your time but, having said that, congratulations on your role in *Hamlet*. May I come down to London and see it?

People

- Mr Bose sounds very decent and, despite being a little serious, is clearly someone who is looking out for your interests. Give him the respect that he's due. One thing that I learnt, perhaps a little late in life, is the fact that you must always be courteous to everyone. Anger does sometimes get in the way. Also make it your business to keep in touch with people.

- I'm not very impressed with the fact that your boss, Mr Khalif Almoun, has spent little time with you. That's how mistakes get made. If your senior managers don't explain things to you, you can't be expected to deliver what's required or to exceed expectations. I take it that your induction was sufficiently detailed. That really is important and it's something that not all organisations do well.

Language

- Unfortunately, corporate life is full of acronyms and you'll (have to) get used to it and them. Personally, I loathe acronyms and, indeed, any jargon. The latter is hard to avoid, but it *doesn't* have to be embraced. Communication is best kept simple. The important thing is that the person or people to whom you're speaking must understand everything you're saying.

- A mistake many professionals often make is to assume that their colleagues, customers, clients and other audiences understand the everyday jargon they use. In most instances, this *isn't* the case and can result in problematic issues. When an individual has difficulty understanding what is being communicated, this can lead him or her forming the wrong conclusion about what was or is being conveyed.

- The danger of jargon is that too often it becomes a crutch, using big-sounding phrases with no meaning to say little (like the three-column list you sent me). There is a big difference between using jargon to illustrate a point and using it to obfuscate one.

- There are some phrases that truly do the language of Shakespeare no good service. Amongst them: 'going forward', 'at the end of the day', 'fairly unique' (it's either unique or it isn't), 'I personally', 'at this moment in time', 'with all due respect', 'absolutely', 'shouldn't of', '24/7', 'cutting-edge', 'leverage' (Arthur please tell them that it's not a verb), 'let's run it up the pole and see what sticks', 'blue sky thinking', 'show me the money' and so on *ad* unfortunately *infinitum*.

- In order to avoid the problems that can arise from using business and/or technical jargon in communications, it is best to simply avoid using it.

Speech-writing
- Writing a speech is not an easy task, although it's great that you've been given an opportunity to shine. Don't worry about making mistakes – we all do – but learn from them.

- Structure is important, as is understanding the person for whom you're writing. That's not always easy and newbies like you are often thrust in the deep end to write a speech without knowing anything about the orator. The primary objective of any speech is to give a message to the audience by conveying a theme and a proposition. For example, if you are delivering a speech at a wedding, you might consider the following themes: importance of family structure, value of marriage, prosperity, continuity and love. The proposition (only one per speech please) might be: 'love lasts'.

- The key to picking a suitable stance and style is evaluating who your speaker's audience will be. The theme and proposition of the speech must relate to the audience and what they already know about the topic. That means that you really *do* need to know what your speaker is like and therefore can't be expected to write the speech blind. Insist on speaking to and getting to know the people for whom you write.

- Start your speech with an attention-grabber such as a question or story to make the audience curious or laugh. Most of all, you want them onside. Using a strong statement at the beginning is also a good idea as long as you can back it up with brilliant examples or logic.

- Structure the speech with clear transitions from one point to another. Many make the mistake of assuming that an audience will be able to follow the speaker's logic. At the same time, don't write in a condescending manner. No audience likes being demeaned or thought of as stupid.

- Stay focused. Many speechwriters get bogged down on one point and lose track of the overall proposition. As you write your speech, keep in mind the proposed audience's perceptions and reactions.

- You're not necessarily an expert on the subject matter, so you do need to talk to one – it doesn't have to be the speaker, but someone who will ensure that you understand the content. Don't forget, your speaker will (and should) add his or her own elements to what you write and, undoubtedly, there will be other 'advisors' who will chip in on content. Too many of those is not a helpful addition but, I fear, you may not be able to dictate terms just yet!

- Your conclusion should be just as strong, if not stronger, than your first paragraph. Write a conclusion that summarises each of your points, relating back to the main theme of your speech. You could end with a strong anecdote or a relevant joke to leave a lasting impression.

- Make the speech dynamic. Engage your audience. Avoid trying to be too flowery in your speech-writing and use simple sentences that your speaker can deliver clearly. Over time, get to know how your speaker delivers phrases and sentences. Follow that and add to that pattern. Discover how your presenter likes to present. Behind a lectern? Strolling about? Bullet points or the whole script word for word? Using a prompting device or not? Big text font? Many politicians and business execs have speechwriters who know everything about their intonation, cadence, patterns and mannerisms.

- Strong speeches usually require an active voice, so remove passive phrases and verbs like 'has', 'had' and 'are'. While keeping your sentences simple, use longer sentences for variety, rhythm and timing. People like rhythmic speeches — much like music, they are easy on the ear. Think of some of the great orators and preachers. Read some of their speeches. Presidential speeches are a great source of phraseology and clever sentences.

- Use quotes sparingly. It's a good idea to include some (but not too many) famous quotes by notable speakers. But use quotes only if they really reinforce a point. And make sure that the quote isn't too obscure. Our American colleague, Professor Wally, quoted Emily Dickinson's *There is Another Sky* to a group of university investors last week. There was a terrible silence. Followed by a gaping void (and many a mouth) when he gave us Alan Ginsberg's *America*. In full.

- Revise and rehearse! No matter how well you think you've written your speech, chances are your speech will still have grammar, punctuation and spelling errors. More importantly, what may sound like a great speech to you may not be so for an average audience. Also be mindful of choice of words, content, structural issues and overall style. Revising is not an easy task. Have your speech edited. Ask Mr Bose for some help here perhaps.

Delivering a speech

- Mr Flattergleich sounds as if he has difficulties in making a speech. (By the way, there is a Dr Flattergleich from Freiburg University who is a specialist on Goethe. I met him at The Goethe Institut in London. I wonder if he's any relation?)

- It's not your job to interfere, but you might recommend to your managers that Mr F could use some presentation training. No shame in that – most execs could do with some. But suggest with care. He is after all your senior by many levels.

- Reading his entire speech from a script may give Mr F confidence and ensure that nothing is forgotten or omitted. However, that is the least desirable option because the speech will sound as if it *is* being read, unless he's very skilled indeed at oratory.

- If Mr F is not confident enough to recite his speech from memory (and that has attendant risks too), then the use of notes is a better option. The notes should consist of the main speech points – a skeleton of thoughts/phrases around which you and he can build the speech. He may refer to his notes occasionally to maintain the thread of the speech, but for the most part he should be able to speak directly to the audience.

Social media
- Actually, young Arthur, I *do* have a BlackBerry now – plus Twitter and Facebook accounts, but rarely use either. They're useful to keep in tune with my students, but 'care' is the watchword in their use.

- Clearly you were left to sink or swim regarding the Twitter affair and that's totally wrong. However, having said that, you really should have had the sense to separate your personal messages from the corporate.

- Apologising for mistakes is essential. Some people and businesses often admit nothing, apologise for nothing and portray an arrogance that does nothing to engage others. Big businesses need to move away from this approach and instead show that they understand how their social media (or, indeed, any) actions affect others. They also have to be willing to follow up. Your error was by and large a training (and perhaps common sense) issue. Establishing an agreed list of acceptable hashtags for corporate tweets could reduce this kind of mistake, although the list would need to be regularly reviewed and updated.

Well, that's enough from me for the moment. I have to prepare for the Farouq and Emir lecture which, as you know, will be harrowing. My subject is 'Sexual Deviancies in Shakespeare's Minor Characters With Particular Reference to the Histories'. No, only joking. It's 'Rhyme and Reason in *Midsummer Night's Dream*'. Wish me luck, dear boy, as I do you.

Yours truly,

Professor Steven Charteris

Chapter Two

"Hell is empty and all the devils are here."

Ariel: *The Tempest* (I, ii) Shakespeare

11

From: Arthur Shilling [arthur.shilling@gammondhopes.com]
Sent: 08/4/2011 19.16 PM GMT
To: Steven Charteris [stevencharteris@staracademy.com]
Subject: Getting better all the time

Steven (may I call you Steve now?)

Thanks very much for your mail – really useful pointers. I should put your thoughts into a communications blog, but I'll keep you a winning secret for a while longer. You should write a book you know! I mean another book, of course.

The preparation for the Chairman's Executive Forum (we've dropped the WISE acronym because nobody could remember what it stood for) is moving on apace. Deaf Knee Hong is OK, despite her bossiness. We're getting on quite well and I've learnt to support her in public and discuss things a little more openly when we're alone. She visibly softens when she comes into contact with Mr Bose, who doesn't really take any notice. He appears preoccupied, although I have to say that he is so supportive of me. Here's a for instance. I had to write a report about an internal conference I'd attended on 'Factoring Finance in Burgeoning Markets with Particular Reference to South America'. Gasp. I wrote up the content as best I could and it came to a very satisfying forty eight pages. Mr Bose asked to see it and pruned the thing by 75%! The communications lot were very impressed because Mr Almoun ran around waving the report shouting, "This is how to write you scurvy knaves. Look at young Arty's work!" I'm obviously in his good books, because he's winking and pointing at me with a finger gun. I went to thank Mr Bose but he just got on with whatever he was doing – never smiling or really acknowledging that he'd done something remarkable. I wanted to tell Mr Almoun that Mr Bose was the real champion, but never got round to it.

For the Chairman's Executive Forum, we have a rich tapestry of material and some excellent feet to tread the stage. As an event host we have ******* ******* from the BBC. Strange to see him in the flesh, because he's tiny but very bright and pleasant. Knows a great deal about a great deal – I suppose that comes with rushing around and talking to the world about matters diplomatique. Seems to want to argue overmuch with Dephne though. Her smile remains fixed. Then we have a bunch of experts arranged by Deaf Knee, who was assisted by someone called Jackie Gershwin, an implant from the event agency. She has the biggest nose that I have ever seen and it really is hard to have a conversation without being mesmerised by said nose. Haven't really got her measure yet (apart from aforesaid nasal capacity) and she just talks across or over me anyway. Mr Bose saw her doing that this morning and he frowned.

Well, let me give you a flavour of the Executive Forum's line-up. We have the Founder and VP of Soluciones Grecitataagncie, an Argentinian future solutions team which measures risk for businesses wanting to sell their services in the region. The gent who's speaking is called Enrique de Cervantes. I really wanted to ask whether he was a relation of the great Miguel, but my Spanish isn't good enough. Dephne called him 'Kipper' but don't ask me why. Then there's an Indian academic called Dr Rashwani and he's a Founder of the Corporate and Research Unit of Murdapor Pradesh (CRUMP) and he also set up the South India Monetary Production Enterprise Region (SIMPER). Very nice chap and makes a great deal of sense on the topic of India's globalisation journey and where the country will be in 2030. Then there's a Fellow in Economics from Oxford who's another chum of Dephne's – a Dr Adrienne Ng. She will address the conference on the matter of China rising, developing and mattering in world economics and politics by 2030. On security, we have our own Head of Group Security and Fraud – Geoffery ******* – who, it is said, was something big in MI6 and looks like every spy should. Very James Bond – you know, a lock of black hair falling over his forehead and hard grey eyes, light grey suit, soft poplin white shirt and dark blue knitted tie, Walther PPK under his jacket… no just kidding, although he might actually have one. I often wish I had a Walther PPK. It'd stop all the pushing on the Underground.

There's also a Secretary of Public Affairs to a former US president and he'll reflect on America's role in the world a decade from now. The undercurrent is whether the USA will remain the world's policeman. Unfortunately, this gent has an alleged cocaine habit and we must be on our mettle, says Deaf Knee with a knowing look.

There are to be two London events, one now and one in several months' time. The current London event is to take place in a trendy hotel in St Martin's Lane and one of the dinners will be in the National Gallery which our company sponsors.

Gotta fly.

Best, Arthur

12

From: Arthur Shilling [arthur.shilling@gammondhopes.com]
Sent: 08/8/2011 07.16 AM GMT
To: Steven Charteris [stevencharteris@staracademy.com]
Subject: Getting harder

Steven

I was invited to attend a rock concert at Wembley, which seems to double as a football ground and rock venue. The company has a box and invites clients to various entertainments. *Take That* was playing on this occasion. Remember Robbie Williams? Of course he's not to be confused with Robin Williams, a mistake made by Mr F. There were twelve of us in the box and all (except me) were very senior clients and top brass from the bank. I was there because of my role with the Chairman's Executive Forum. I was naturally a bit shy, but everyone was pretty drunk so it made no difference whether I said much or not. I did begin to explain to one director of a major food company my theory of whether Shakespeare wrote 'his' plays, but it was a short-lived conversation and I believe that I lost his attention after explaining my view on Bacon's knowledge of law. His response was to look at me red-eyed and say something that I don't even know how to spell.

Had a headache the next morning, but believe that I might be destined for higher things one day. The Chairman's opening address has been finalised and is with his office now for approval. The script had to be seen by no less than twelve people, each of whom made verbal comments – never any written ones (cowardly eh?). The speech starts like this: "Built on trust, respect and goodwill, a good relationship eases the exchange of information on expectations and therefore enables successful cooperation. As time goes on and the challenges become no less difficult, more so actually, we must better understand the world around us, not just from a banking position…" Mr F accosted me in the lift and talked about the speech. "Ze top bwass are pleased Arssur, and while I feel that the overview is sound, the dittle of the second half is not kvite the same level of agreeable banter as might be found in ze first – alzough the basic tenet of new vorld order for ze 2030s might be stretching credulity…" I excused myself and, face burning, got off at the 12th floor instead of the 52nd.

I met the Chairman briefly at a meeting to discuss his Executive Forum. He did say hello but not a lot else. He listens intently to people, sometimes looking directly at the speaker, sometimes to the mid-distance through his vast eyrie windows. He has a habit of asking questions which nobody wants to, or can, answer. Out of the blue he asked, "How many users of Facebook are there worldwide?", to which Mr Bose answered, "689 million or close to". The Chairman nodded and everyone else looked admiringly at Mr Bose. "And Twitter?" Again Mr Bose answered and not in the least arrogantly, "175 million". We thought that the Chairman would move on but he didn't. "Landline telephones?" I knew the answer to that one and said tentatively, "1.2 billion". Everyone looked at me, including Mr Bose. The Chairman said, "And there are around 2 billion Internet users with 5.3 billion mobile phones in circulation. The global population's what, around 7 billion? OK. Let's have that in the speech please."

I walked out on air. Mr Bose left with his phone glued to his ear. He was absorbed in something other than the numbers of telephones in the world.

Best

Arthur

13

From: Arthur Shilling [arthur.shilling@gammondhopes.com]
Sent: 08/19/2011 22.16 PM GMT
To: Steven Charteris [stevencharteris@staracademy.com]
Subject: Hard times

Steven

The play rehearsals are going great guns and even the chap with the lisp has smartened up his speech a little. One imagines that he couldn't quite do a rendition of 'She sells seashells…' but he's getting better. Graham Graveling (my best chum) is playing Leontes and he's very good indeed. We go off for a pie and a pint after rehearsals and we share more or less the same (slightly drunk) views of the world.

You will have to judge my modest Horatio when you see it. Ophelia has changed in the sense that playing her now is an Afro Caribbean girl who's very good indeed, but doesn't quite fit as Polonius' daughter. Nonetheless, we're all getting on famously. Linda Nookles (pronounced Nighclay, not Knuckles) is our director/producer. She's in the Private Bank and speaks as if she has marbles in her mouth. I wanted to ask if in fact she did because Demosthenes is said to have practised oratory with stones in his mouth.

For the departmental team meeting we had been asked to prepare something interesting that had little to do with work or banking. My subject was 'William Shakespeare was the most influential person who ever lived'. I put some greats (including Jesus, Muhammad, Newton, Freud and Lennon) to one side in my presentation, and explained how influence should be measured – not just something that's counted in literary references or Google hits, but something less tangible, more magical. I explained and demonstrated how Shakespeare's words make the world shiver and everyday things vibrate. I brushed aside my usual restraint and spoke with vigour and ease. I pointed out that every writer of note over the last 350 years or so has been influenced by the work of Shakespeare. Mrs Sourdough thought that I was being irreligious and frowned. Someone else (I think from Wolverhampton) asked to which Lennon I was referring.

After the meeting, I was approached by several people who wondered if they could ask my advice with regards to *their* speeches! They had, they said, been fascinated by the number of words that Shakespeare had coined, like abstemious, accused, addiction, amazement, arouse, auspicious, anchovy… here's me telling you! Anyway, they wanted some input on how best to use quotes to support main speech points. I whisper to myself, paraphrasing that wonderful line of Malvolio: "Be not afraid of greatness Arthur: some are born great, some achieve greatness, and some have greatness thrust upon 'em." It doesn't scan as well of course.

Best

Arthur Shilling
(professional writer and adviser to the banking community)

14

From: Arthur Shilling [arthur.shilling@gammondhopes.com]
Sent: 08/23/2011 23.16 PM GMT
To: Steven Charteris [stevencharteris@staracademy.com]
Subject: Harder times

Steven

Mr Almoun zipped by my desk and screeched to a halt. "Chairman's gig is tomorrow, right? Ready?" I began to answer but, before I could, he said, "Fanbloodytastic! The eyes of the world will be on you!" Then he scooted off, waving suggestively at Mrs Sourdough who blushed scarlet. She was heard to say, "Really, how rude, or some such thing."

Am I ready? Well, it's not all down to me of course. Dephne Hong is the architect on this one and she hasn't missed a detailed trick. The production company folk have been hard work of course. I say 'of course' because the people here say that all production and agency folk are quite hard work. They earn more than we do and wander round our offices in jeans when suits and occasional ties are our *modus operandi*. They also seem very good at passing the hard work back to us. I don't really care for Ms Raspberry Jenkins, the event's producer. She's arrogant and doesn't listen to anything anyone says unless it's Deaf Knee. Gloria Mishmash from our PR department almost sprang across a meeting room table when Raspberry shrugged her shoulders about some question that she (Gloria) had asked. And Jackie Gershwin, she of the big nose and from the same agency, just waves away any questions I have about speakers.

The process of the Chairman's Forum has been complicated too, as is anything involving the Chairman. I have to say that I am reasonably proud of all the miles of corridor that I have dutifully trudged, all the volumes of memos and reminders and the 'just jot that in an email to me' notes that I have solemnly delivered, mostly without assistance. Plus all the weight of institutional gravitas that I have played a small part in bearing. I've been party to all the last minute conference calls with each speaker or contributor. We've had visitations from thingy (our event facilitator) from the BBC whose name I mustn't mention and we've had the Chairman's office phoning and requesting secretarial and PA briefings *ad infinitum*. Dephne asked me out for a drink which I enjoyed, although the saké that she made me put away went straight to my head and I told jokes to which I couldn't recall the punchlines. Deaf Knee laughed anyway.

The play is becoming hard work what with the late nights I'm keeping at the office. I have to confess to losing my temper with Mr Lisping Hamlet. A small group of the cast were waiting for the director, La Nookles, to find her notes when a discussion about education arose and our friend began thus: "You can't tell me that collegeth and univerthitieth are all going downhill. Thath the governmenth propanganda and, of courth, the rithe in feeth." I'd had enough and told him someone with such an impediment shouldn't be onstage, particularly in the title role. There was a bit of a hush after that and the group drifted several ways. I was spoken to by Ms Nookles and I, forgetting what I had learnt, said, "Sorry Ms Nuckles."

I went up to Hamlet to apologise. He was decent and we shook hands. He told me that he'd spent his childhood positioning the tip of his tongue against the rear of his top teeth, right up against the gum line. He said that, for the most part, the effect produced a sound not dissimilar to that of a slowly emptying balloon. It was, he said, awkward and strange-sounding and elicited more attention than the original lisp. But, he added, the lisp was predominantly a result of nerves. We went for a drink after rehearsals and I tried some strong Suffolk ale which I much enjoyed.

Last minute arrangements for the Executive Forum. So and so's plane will be late, such and such has lost his something or other, a man nobody's heard of asked which hotel the event is at, some people have misplaced their joining instructions, others want to bring their wives, children or mistresses.

We've designed and built a website for the event. I can't claim much responsibility although I have learnt a great deal in the process. We are having problems with people's food requirements: meat or no meat, gluten-free options, vegetarian choices, with and without eggs, dairy free, fat free, kosher, halal and so on. Nightmare. Anyway, fingers crossed.

Thanks by the way for the copy of the newspaper cutting featuring Mrs C walking free. She has a lot of supporters, doesn't she? Really pleased for you. And her.

Kind regards

Arthur

15

From: Arthur Shilling [arthur.shilling@gammondhopes.com]
Sent: 08/30/2011 21.16 PM GMT
To: Steven Charteris [stevencharteris@staracademy.com]
Subject: Phew!

Steven

The Executive Forum was a great, great success! The Chairman gave his speech *extempore*, but used every single fact and argument that I had created (and in the right order!). Many of the senior executives congratulated me. Mr Bose caught my eye at one point and just nodded gently. I could have wept, not least because the music used to walk attendees in after lunch was *American Idiot* by Green Day rather than the extract from Grieg's *Peer Gynt* that I had chosen.

The event, as I think I told you, was basically split into four areas of interest: People, Behaviour, Environment and Business. Half a day for each topic. It went very smoothly despite the expected panic when a number of speakers were late or when an Australian professor decided to change each and every PowerPoint slide ten minutes before kick-off. Overall, though, all was more or less well. The delegates seemed to enjoy themselves and networked nicely.

There was one small hiccup and that was in the Environment session. We had Professor Wally Nibblet, Senior Fellow in Environmental Studies from the University of Virginia. His thesis is that facts show an argument against climate alarmism, i.e. this is no time to panic. Opposing this view was a Dr Petrie Alleyn from the Department of Physics at Oxford, whose claim is that with regard to climate change, this *is* a perfect time to panic.

It all began well enough, both giving decent and well-argued presentations although, in hindsight, there were one or two barbs particularly from our American friend. After the presentations came a Q&A session and the stage was joined by a Matt Prince, who is Director of The Growth and Human Advisory Scenario Team Link Institution (GHASTLI). Matt took issue with the American and Dr Alleyn, sensing blood, bared his teeth. Matt and the doc tried to beat the prof with (I have to say) weak argument.

This went on for a bit, aided and abetted by our friend from the BBC who, up till then, had done a good job of facilitating everything. Suddenly the American shouted, "You are both extraordinarily stupid and I don't really want to give you or you (now pointing at audience) any more of my valuable time. Stuff the fee. I'm outta here." And with that he gathered his substantial paperwork and left, dropping documents and prophylactics as he fled. Some in the audience tittered. All looked to see what reaction the Chairman would have, but he waited impassively, arms folded, for the event to continue – which it did without further hitch.

The dinner at the National Gallery went well and I attended. To my right was a manager from Birmingham. We were sitting amongst some of the world's finest art. On the walls in our immediate vicinity were paintings by Tintoretto – beautiful and worth studying for hours. I enquired of my neighbour if he liked the work. "Hate all paintings me," was his abrupt reply. "Sorry," said I, "All paintings?" I must have looked and sounded shocked, for I was, because he smiled the smile of the arrogantly ignorant (how could this be a bank manager?) and said, "All paintings. All absolutely crap. Give me a good photograph any time me." That was that really. I ventured a question about his family, but I really wasn't interested and spent the rest of the evening talking to the fellow to my left who was something senior in Rio. His English wasn't that stable, but at least we could talk reasonably well about the art and he agreed that it was 'very good'. At the end of dinner I did turn to the twit from Birmingham and bade him farewell. He thrust a card at me and I fully imagined that it would say Geoffery Sitwell, Art Hater and Book Burner on it. I smiled, bid him *adieu* and tossed his card on the table where it was lost amongst the detritus.

Yours

Arthur

16

From: Arthur Shilling [arthur.shilling@gammondhopes.com]
Sent: 09/06/2011 04.16 AM GMT
To: Steven Charteris [stevencharteris@staracademy.com]
Subject: The play's the thing

Steven

I'm really sorry that you couldn't come down to see *Hamlet*, but I do understand that your workload (and Mrs C) forestalled the best laid plans. Never mind. There *will* be a next time but you were missed. Raspberry Jenkins, event producer most arrogant, did actually come along but she has no idea of Shakespeare's language, the ebb, the flow, the highs and the lows. She prefers Arcade Fire's music, whoever *they* are. She comes from Exeter. "Arthur," she said. "Art, this is cool and Hamlet's muv in the play is way cool." Believe it or not (and I don't), she got a good degree from King's in anthropology.

My landlady, Victoria Holyhead, came along too and she was very complimentary. Mrs H, divorcée and gorgeous, is a film and TV makeup artist. She's worked on many TV programmes and feature films. She's abroad for much of the time, but always asks after my welfare and progress. Her eyes twinkle with fun and general naughtiness and she has this amazingly bouncy red hair. Why Mr Holyhead bogged off I have no idea because she's wonderful. I've learnt loads of makeup tips, such as how to create bruises, cuts and warts. I managed to paint a horrific wound on my forehead with bits of glass sticking out and the next day I did go into work with it all still on but had to quickly clean up my act since we had an unscheduled departmental meeting and Mr Bose told me that my facial alterations were not conducive to good business or career prospects.

Anyway, the play: the performances (six shows in all) took place in the company's theatre. Yes, we have our own and it's fully equipped. Mind you, it's also used for conferences and presentations and in fact I've been asked to produce an event in it for the Private Bank. But more of that anon.

Was the play a success? I'd say that, on the whole, it was and I believe that this was a generally held view. The musicians were a tad out of sorts for some reason and the aimless whisper of the two flutes sounded not unlike the wind whipping across the top of an empty Coke bottle. The piano on occasion sounded much as if a cat was chasing a mouse across the keys. That aside, all went well. We ran at just over three hours which isn't bad for a *Hamlet* that had not had its script edited. Our hero did perhaps race a little (actually a lot) but his lisp – magically gone! As for me, I think that you'd have been proud even though my tights did sag at the knee. The play's poster was for some reason a picture of what was meant to have been a bowl of cherries. However, it looked more like a pile of stones hovering over a dark grey halo or an old tyre. But, onwards and upwards.

At a committee meeting on the development of the company's main Intranet site (content), there was made mention of so many different aspects of business terminology that my head did spin. Then references were made to great authors and tomes, of which I had heard none. I decided that I could no longer practice bluff. To bluff is exhausting after a while and I have quickly learnt it was easier to simply reply with a question – as one of my peer group did in one of my literature tutorials back in the day, saying "I know what Keats means to me, but what do *you* think of her?" I have decided that I need to educate myself a little in the ways and mores of business.

As a celebration of the Chairman's Executive Forum's success, Deaf Knee took the team out for dinner. There were around sixteen people in all, some from my department and some from the agency. There was someone from the venue as well, although she kept leaving the table to make or receive phone calls. Bad form I thought. Unfortunately, the restaurant Dephne chose wasn't a great hit. It was a new Japanese resort trying too hard to be 'in'. Waiters presented us with small dishes of things that were meant to amuse the palette. None of them amused mine. Most dishes consisted of rolled up things the colour of a corn plaster floating in a muddy puddle of some sauce or other topped with a smattering of bright green. Even when a waiter explained that a particular dish was raw Atlantic swordfish, it looked and tasted exactly the same as every other dish, including dessert. Dephne resorted to drinking much saké as, unfortunately, did I.

I have to produce a speech for Mr F and he's asked for some help in delivery. Nobody knows whether that's for me to do or an external specialist. He wants/needs some presentation and media training because he's heavily involved with Grammond Hopes' purchasing of a South African bank and will need to acquaint the press with what's going on. I think he might be petrified. My first speech for him on 'Moral Terpitude in a Balanced Marketplace' was a veritable disaster, so this one had better be good. Mind you, 'Moral Terpitude' was not really my fault since I had no real briefing and little help (dear Mr Bose was abroad at the time). The speech that I have to help with now is about sustainability. I had to attend a meeting involving the company's sustainability gurus: the Group Environmental Advisor (who is on loan from the WWF) and the Head of Sustainable Development. Each dislikes the other intensely and it was a tough meeting. I did learn though that the world will indeed end with a nuclear holocaust, so that was reassuring. It's also apparent that banks end up financing weapon purchases and probably terrorism (not directly of course but certainly indirectly). Anyway, the meeting was barbed with acrimony. Our chap banged on about how rubbish he thought the WWF was and sneered at the alleged concentration on pandas (a bit harsh I thought).

It looks as if my troupe will be doing another Shakespeare in a few months. It could be *Midsummer Night's Dream* which would be great fun. You thought my Bottom wasn't half bad in my first year, so I might have a bash at that if I can.

Arthur

17

From: Arthur Shilling [arthur.shilling@gammondhopes.com]
Sent: 09/10/2011 09.16 AM GMT
To: Steven Charteris [stevencharteris@staracademy.com]
Subject: Briefs

Steven

I've just taken the brief for the Private Bank conference. There are actually two. One will be here in London in our conference auditorium and is for media and financial writers – about vision, projections, new products… that kind of thing. Later in the year there'll be another for clients (very, very rich people) in Monaco, with very high production values and a budget to match I think. Deaf Knee is leading both. Hurray.

The briefing session was chaotic. Nobody had prepared anything so the 'client', a Swedish lady (Stephanie Gorgoson) of vast stature and with Louboutin high heels spoke at length about the proposed content. La Hong and I genuinely didn't understand what Stephanie was really saying, although her shoes were historic. She has a deep voice and a huge gap in her top front teeth. It makes her look like a huge Scandinavian pixie. Unlike a pixie, she has no sense of humour. Or sense of fact. Every time our side asked a question like: "How many people will there be attending the London event?" we received odd and vague answers such as, "Probable one hunnerd. Or two. Maybe. Sree if all goes fine, huh?" Even Dephne was at a loss. The auditorium only holds two hundred and fifty people and H&S (health and safety!) forbids any standing. "H&S is the. Bane of our lives," says Deaf Knee.

Anyway, we muddled through the meeting. Stephanie's sidekick is a Shirl Girlinawhirl. I don't think that's her real name but that's what it sounded like. She's Australian and insists upon being called Shirl even though her name's Beverley. Her contribution to the meeting was to say "Right, right", or "What do you think about that, guys?" La Hong asked for a written brief and I remembered little about the meeting – having been mesmerised by Scandinavian heights, gap teeth and Australian nose twitching. I suggested another meeting in two days' time at which we could go through the written brief. Surprisingly, everyone agreed, not least because a proposal for both events has to go before the Private Bank's CEO in a couple of weeks' time.

Art (as in Garfunkel). What do you think?

18

From: Arthur Shilling [arthur.shilling@gammondhopes.com]
Sent: 09/15/2011 02.16 AM GMT
To: Steven Charteris [stevencharteris@staracademy.com]
Subject: The Dream

We've had the first auditions for *Midsummer Night's Dream*. I was keen to audition for one of the mechanicals, although Percy Adler, one of the lighting technicians, did think that I should go for one of the leads. "Better than that lisping prat," he murmured. I'm not absolutely sure if that was in recognition of my prowess or the sibilance of Mr Hamlet. I did audition for Bottom and I think that you'd have been pleased. I was asked to read for Theseus, but I think he's a dullard and said no. I was then asked to read for Flute, which I did, and wondered then if I should have gone for

Puck, a marvelous part of course. However, the nimble skipping that I would have been obliged to undertake probably ruled me out and I thought no more of being Oberon's puppet faerie.

The woman from Accounts Forwarding who read Titania is wonderful – in all regards. Long, (real) black hair and pale of cheek, with willowy legs and pert... enough, perhaps... suffice to say that I am in love. She looked my way not once. Her rendition of the soft words when Bottom (hopefully me!) rests in her comfortable lap was sublime:

> "Be kind and courteous to this gentleman;
> Hop in his walks, and gambol in his eyes;
> Feed him with apricocks, and dewberries,
> With purple grapes, green figs, and mulberries;
> The honey-bags steal from the humble-bees,
> And, for night-tapers, crop their waxen thighs,
> And light them at the fiery glow-worm's eyes,
> To have my love to bed and to arise;
> And pluck the wings from painted butterflies,
> To fan the moon-beams from his sleeping eyes."

Ah. Whenever I shall see purple grapes I shall think of her. Unfortunately, the role of Oberon is definitely going to this guy from Trusts who is about ten feet tall and has rugged Sean Connery Bond looks with a deep and mellifluous baritone voice. No. My Bottom is good enough for me and, besides, it's a wonderful role, particularly if Miss Accounts Forwarding gets the part of Titania!

I have spent a fair amount of time with Mr F helping him in to get into better shape for his major sustainability presentation. We did some voice exercises at his request, but that didn't last long because when I tried 'Peter Piper picked...", Mr F didn't get past two words before stopping and looking lost. He speaks German quite a lot during our sessions (possibly because he now knows that I speak passable German) and the script for his presentation is taking an age to formulate – objectives, proposition, tone and so on. He is insisting on swathes of PowerPoint and wants to stand on stage looking at the screen while basically reading his whole script from it.

A bit tired now.

Regards

Art (So what *do* you think of Art? People in the office quite like it although Mr Bose clearly does not.)

19

From: Arthur Shilling [arthur.shilling@gammondhopes.com]
Sent: 09/20/2011 05.16 AM GMT
To: Steven Charteris [stevencharteris@staracademy.com]
Subject: Scandinavian and others

Steven

I think I'll revert to Arthur because some in the department took to putting an 'F' on the front of my shortened name. I may have to resort to the use of my middle name for a while, but I'll do that only in dire straits. Mind you, when the teasing was rife, Mr Bose just stood up at his desk and a hush descended, one almost of awe. Everyone went back to work and there were surreptitious but nervous glances at Mr B even when he had resumed his seat.

I went with Deaf Knee for our second meeting concerning the Private Bank Media Conference (as it will be called, to be distinct from the Private Bank Customer Congress which is the Monaco event). We were joined by the gap-toothed Scandinavian and her monosyllabic Australian cousin. The written brief was appalling. There was no real objective, no indication of content, thousands of acronyms, jargon galore, no budget profile, no audience profile (just 'the media and advisory companies'). We were saved from Ms Hong erupting (and, I have to say, I would have applauded her) when the meeting door was flung open and a tall, slim man with mad, sticking-up hair and wild eyes behind thick-lensed spectacles rushed in. He was wearing red braces and his suit trousers went up to mid chest. He, I found out, is the Private Bank's CEO. He sat down and looked at the brief, gazed oddly at Miss Scandinavia and proceeded to explain in prime detail all the information we needed to go forth and prepare a response on both events. He then apologised profusely to his two colleagues for not having made the briefs clear to them. He stood, bowed slightly and left the room. Suddenly we four were bosom buddies and we ate all the biscuits.

Arthur (or my middle name – Sheridan – what do you think?)

20

From: Arthur Shilling [arthur.shilling@gammondhopes.com]
Sent: 09/25/2011 05.16 AM GMT
To: Steven Charteris [stevencharteris@staracademy.com]
Subject: Mr F

Steven

Mr F and his presentation style (or non-existent presentation style) are doing my head in. He always finishes our sessions with "*Meine Tür ist immer geöffneter Artur*" ("My door is always open, Arthur") and this is really odd because his door is never open and he likes one to knock and wait upon which he shouts "*Hereingekommen!*" ("Come in!") and you do. It's all very ordered in his office and the pencils (never used) sit point up in a special holder. If Mr F tripped and fell on his desk, he'd kill himself with fifty pencil points.

We always have to go through my week or day or anything else that takes his muse. He sees himself as a Freudian therapist and asks embarrassing questions like: "*So was denken Sie an Herrn oder Fräulein so und so?*" ("So what do you think of Mr or Miss So and So?") In fact, 'so' is a favourite word of his, although he too likes 'Shakespeam' as he likes to pronounce the Bard's name. We discuss MND from time to time, one of his favourites apparently. The other day he quoted (badly) at length:

"I know a bank where the wild thyme blows,
Where oxlips and the nodding violet grows,
Quite over-canopied with luscious woodbine,
With sweet musk-roses and with eglantine.
There sleeps Titania sometime of the night,
Lull'd in these flowers with dances and delight."

Except this is the sort of thing he did to murder Oberon (II, i):

"I know a bangt vare ze vilde time blows,
Vare oxslips und ze noddingt wiolet goes,
Kvite ober-kan-opie mit luffly voodbine,
Mit sveet, sveet musk-roses ant mit eglantine.
Zare," (and Mr F pointed somewhere on the floor) "sleeps
Titania zumtime of de nide,
Lull-erd in deese flowers mit dance und delide!"

And then he bowed from the neck and, if we had been standing on wooden, rather than deep-carpeted floor, I swear that he would have clicked his heels. He paused for a beat and then said, "*Sie müssen meine Zeit, Artur zu vergeuden wirklich stoppen. Wir müssen mit der Rede an erhalten.*" ("You really have to stop wasting my time Arthur. We must get on with the speech.")

And so, apart from a few more occasional quotes, we did get on with the speech and his presentation. He would sometimes pause, look out over his Docklands view and murmur Lysander's famous line from Act I, scene i: "The course of true love never did run smooth," although of course it didn't sound like that. Now that I've won the part, I am learning Bottom's lines with his occasional 'help'. He avidly wants to assist and listens without demur to the likes of Act IV, i:

"I have had a most rare vision
I have had a dream
Past the wit of man to say what dream it was."

I asked why he didn't go for a small part in a play and he just stared out of the picture window watching the ants that were people and said nothing. He nodded and I wondered what had happened to stop a clearly gifted romantic from following what he clearly wanted to do.

Steven, strange to say, I'm really enjoying this job. Really.

Very best as always

Arthur

>

From: Steven Charteris [stevencharteris@staracademy.com]
Sent: 09/27/2011 08.16 AM GMT
To: Arthur Shilling [arthur.shilling@gammondhopes.com]
Subject: Getting better all the time

Arthur

Getting Better All the Time is one of my favourite Beatles' tracks (that and *Strawberry Fields* and actually, while we're at it, the second side of *Abbey Road*). Congratulations on all fronts and I truly am sorry that I couldn't get to your show. I'm delighted though that it went so very well indeed and as you are fond of saying, onwards and upwards!

You are learning valuable lessons.

Successful cooperation

- Clarity contributes to sustaining good relationships because people learn to trust each other when they have the same

understanding of roles, responsibilities and levels
of authority.

- Social life with a business is important. Next time you're
invited to something, learn a little about your fellow guests
beforehand and consider what might interest them. Most
senior business people don't really want to discuss their work
or yours when they're out of the office and particularly if it's
time to relax. Go easy on the booze even if others don't. You
never know when you'll need a clear head.

Speeches
- Your Mr F is a romantic. English isn't his first language and
that may be difficult for him. Whatever the scenario, you
must still be courteous. The key for you is clarity – make
everything you say (and do) plain. Remember, you're new
and you're there to learn. Also remember that some people
will stand by you in your darkest hour (not many alas, but
that's life), others will walk away and some, a select few, will
march towards you and become firm friends.

- Getting useful and relevant facts in a speech is important and
it's clear that your Chairman is on the ball. Be prepared for him
to put your speech to one side (having gone through it many
times I suspect) and deliver his twenty minutes without notes
or the dreaded PowerPoint. As you intimate, PowerPoint can
strangle any presentation and bore the pants off an audience.

- It's fantastic that your speechwriting prowess is growing
apace and I'm proud of the fact that you did well with your
Shakespeare piece. Using quotes with care in speeches is
absolutely fine. Contemplating Shakespeare's ability to sneak

into everyday conversation is a marvel. I have often said, as you will recall, that if an individual doesn't care about Othello, Hamlet or Macbeth, then he or she probably won't care about any character in any book ever. The fact that there are so many who don't care is depressing.

- If your first speech written for Mr F was less than satisfactory (you don't really say how or why), don't fret but consider how *you* can improve. If you're going to write more speeches for him, as it seems you are, then try and get to know more about his thinking and presentation style.

Common barriers to communication

- In essence, anything that prevents understanding of a message is a barrier to communication. However, these barriers may not always be physical but can be psychological as well. Here are some common problems:

   Perception – how we perceive another person can affect how we interpret messages from them; for example, someone who does not articulate clearly or who talks too fast and in a flustered way or whose first language is not English, can cause us to dismiss them or anything they say as unimportant.

   Culture – a person's culture, background and attendant bias or prejudices can affect their reception and interpretation of a message and interfere with the communication process.

   Noise – it may sound stupidly simple, but environmental noise pollution can hinder clear communication. (Remember when you couldn't concentrate because of cafeteria noise?)

Attitude – focusing only on ourselves and our personal feelings can seriously hinder communication. This can take the form of defensiveness, superiority or just plain ego.

Environment – bright lights, unusual sights, other stimuli or even attractive people nearby eating cheese and onion crisps – all can provide unwelcome distractions which interfere with the effectiveness of the communication process. A student of mine often finds it hard to focus on *Henry IV* Part II when Deidre Davenport is sitting opposite in a tutorial, or as in the case of Jefferson Collinbrooke (remember him?), who became a complete wreck when Pete Dellinghose walked in.

Message – this occurs when people focus on the facts instead of the ideas behind the message. This isn't always a bad thing because it's sometimes hard to do both, but the thinking behind the thinking is important.

Non-verbal behaviours

- In many instances, non-verbal behaviour can help to improve channels of communication. One of the best ways to do this is with eye contact: this signals interest in the person or people to whom you're talking and it will increase your credibility as well as improve the flow of communication.

- Facial expressions are also powerful cues for transmitting messages – for example, smiling generally encourages people to react more favourably and people will want to listen to smilers more, although do use some sense here – smiling isn't always appropriate to the subject matter.

- Body postures can express a great deal – we communicate more than you realise by the way we move while talking, so use these non-verbal indicators to your advantage. Although you'll recall Professor Auschtell skipping over-frequently and that wasn't much help in his Divinity lectures. But being serious here, leaning forward, for example, does communicate interest and approachability to others, whereas speaking with your body faced away indicates a lack of respect or interest in the other person.

- Please don't forget the importance of listening.

Preparing briefs
- When preparing a brief, avoid jargon, nonsensical phrases and acronyms. Include facts (without assumptions or embellishments). Use plain English and include as much detail as possible. It's easier and quicker for the recipient to cut out the superfluous rather than have to fill in some gaps. Whether you need a creative brief, web brief, copy brief or even an event brief – here's a useful checklist to help make sure nothing gets missed:

  - Include a short summary about your company or department and its products and services. Try to include something about your brand, its personality and philosophy, as well as its place in the market place. This might be just as useful for an *internal* brief as one to an external supplier. Suggest where the reader can find more appropriate detail, but be specific instead of just pointing in a vague direction to broad chunks on the Internet.

    – Talk about competitor products and services as relevant. What marketing activity are they doing and are they doing it better? Include examples and/or weblinks.

    – The brief has to state *precisely* and concisely what is required. Most don't and, particularly with events, briefs can be unclear. Many briefs don't say clearly enough *why* something is being briefed.

    – A brief must describe the target audience for the communication (or event, campaign, video, website). Why is that particular audience being targeted? Describe why you think this audience needs the information you want to disseminate.

    – Are there any key assumptions being made about what the audience already understands or knows?

    – How will you measure the effectiveness of this activity? What will success look like?

    – It's much easier for people to respond to a brief if you give them some idea of budget.

Arguments

- If you witness arguments between senior colleagues or guests, there is little you can do apart from remaining courteous yourself. You can possibly attempt to change the subject or move the topic along in a meeting, but that's not easy if you're the junior party. Onstage of course you can do little. Sometimes facilitators will wear an earpiece so that the producer can give instructions. Of course, some healthy argument onstage is good, but it does need managing.

- With topics that are likely to cause controversy – such as sustainability or global warming – arguments are likely to occur and the facilitator or event's chair can be briefed accordingly. I remember when the University invited Kelly Softkind, a senior analyst on the subject of socially responsible investment, to take part in a debate ('Should companies take moral responsibilities seriously or only for the purposes of the bottom line?') with Terry Ustinhouse, a director of Friends of a Frying Earth. Ms Softkind all but decapitated Mr Ustinhouse with a microphone stand simply because he wouldn't give way to her beliefs. We had to call an ambulance as I remember.

- Your dinner companion at the National Gallery, who didn't care for paintings, sounds pretty dreadful I agree. But you were there in a hosting mode and therefore courtesy has to rule the day. There will many an occasion when you will be faced with inconsiderate, ignorant, boorish people or some with different mores to your own. If asked to take sides or offer a view of someone in your business, be careful – these things have a nasty habit of backfiring.

I do recall going to a drinks function at the Central Hall in The National Gallery and then on to dinner in the Barry Rooms. This must have been five or six years ago and it was to mark the publication of *Oh Words Are Simply Not Enough* by Professor Susan Mingle. The affair was pleasant enough but there were two Provosts from a Hungarian university who became outrageously drunk and rather abusive about the art of Turner. Michael Prominto, the event's organiser, had them turfed out. The day was ruined because the Hungarian university was funding Mingle's research – or wasn't, as it turned out. So one does have to be careful. It might be best to keep your personal opinions to yourself.

By and large, Arthur, everything seems to be going swimmingly for you and I'm truly delighted. Don't be over-confident and certainly not arrogant. I look forward to learning more of Mr Flattergleich's speeches and their improvements. By the by, is your Zalautha Derong – the cheese and pickle sandwich merchant – related to Barry Derong? If so, that's an extraordinary coincidence because he's here studying literature and is also, like you, something of a thesp. However, he needs to understand that Dickens is to be absorbed, not read once and discarded.

Mrs Charteris sends her best as, of course, do I.

Professor Steven Charteris

Chapter Three

"My heart aches and a drowsy numbness pains
My sense, as though of hemlock I had drunk."

Ode to a Nightingale, John Keats

21

From: Arthur Shilling [arthur.shilling@gammondhopes.com]
Sent: 10/03/2011 10.16 AM GMT
To: Steven Charteris [stevencharteris@staracademy.com]
Subject: Confusions

Steven

Thank you again for your tips. Very helpful and I do take them all to heart. There's a book in this, you know, although I'd probably get into terrible trouble!

I'm busy. Jenny Barstiff, my co-newbie in the department (along with Deidre Sissons from Manchester who sits directly behind me) is clearly not enjoying all of her duties and both Mr Bose and Mrs Sourdough are becoming quite irritated at her adherence to no timetables, schedules or deadlines. Mr Derek Rattles (you'll recall – our Head of EMEA Communications) does like Jenny however and she exists under his wing, although Mrs Sourdough keeps saying that "it'll only lead to trouble or some such terrible thing". Mrs S was also heard to mutter with heavy innuendo, "I wonder what they do at lunchtime? Have lunch? Or some such thing." The 'some such thing' was said with such a leer that her ruby red lipstick stuck to her teeth, an effect that even my makeup artist landlady would have been hard pressed to match in making someone up to look like a zombie with blood on their gnashers.

I do quite like Jenny and the fact that she's always happy. She is, I think, a frustrated ballerina for she is always pirouetting and standing on the edge of her toes. Her bounciness grates when one is trying to concentrate and she asks me for a fair amount of help which I do tend to offer – the result of which is that I don't leave the office until after eight each evening. Mr Bose has noticed and quiet words are being had all round.

Mr Goodenhardt from the US (the one who wants Mr Flattergleich's job as Group Head of Communications) is spending more and more time in London. He chairs vast numbers of strategy meetings, one of which I attended recently. It was all no nonsense and 'woe betide you if you said something slightly left-field or not absolutely pertaining to the topic in hand' type of thing. I was asked to comment on the Chairman's Executive Forum and, as I was about to speak up, there came the sound of singing from the next meeting room. Something like, "A maid again I never shall be / Till apples grow on an orange tree". Everyone stopped fidgeting or, as in my case, speaking, to listen. The voice was celestial, beautiful and, as it trilled, we were all (ten or so souls) mesmerised. Mr G however was incensed that his meeting had been hijacked and, as the singer sang, "I wish, I wish, but it's all in vain / I wish I were a maid again", that did it. Mr Goodenhardt rushed to the meeting room door, yanked it open and goose-stepped to the door of the room next door and that too was wrenched asunder. We all listened with care for the eruption, but came there none. All we heard was a quick glottal-stopped singer and soft murmuring.

After a few moments, Mr G came back and his face was redder than a juicy, freshly-cut watermelon. Without comment or ado, he continued to chair the meeting, but now with a distracted softness that did little to assuage people's anxieties about contributing accurate and appropriate information.

The Chairman is keen to get an update on the next Executive Forum and I wrote some pointers for Deaf Knee Hong about the speakers and topics. Much is the same as the first event, but one or two of the London contributors can't attend the New York gig. The production company people say 'gig' as if what we're doing is rock and roll. They say 'rock and roll' a great deal too as if the phrase was a verb. They're being very pleasant to me now because they consider me a 'somebody' with perhaps some influence. Although Raspberry Jenkins (Welsh you know) is still cool (but not in a cool way). I still get talked over on occasion, although Deaf Knee does say, "I. I want. I want to hear what. What Arthur has. Has to say." She then puts up an imperious hand and all conversation ceases until I've had my small say. The only problem is that if what I have to say isn't terribly interesting, then I feel a bit foolish. When this first happened, I did blush prettily but now I marshal my courage and thoughts before venturing forth. Deaf Knee most definitely regards me as one of the core event team now and I do believe that she's saying good things about me to Jez Staffordshire and co.

Mr Goodenhardt is mightily fed up, however, because I'm going with the Executive Forum to New York and Jenny Barstiff isn't – although why she should even be considered for the trip I have no idea whatsoever! Whenever I now see Mr G in a corridor or lift, he scowls and mutters under his breath. His normally sleek looks are beginning to show signs of disarray. Jenny still skips all over the place and she still likes me and says things like, "Way to go Arty!" as a total non-sequitur before displaying a quick *piqué en arabesque* or a *demi-plié*.

But, New York City beckons! Have never been, so I've bought a book of American lexicons. I'm trying to remain unexcited on the outside, but am really pleased. I've got my suitcase out already. It has wheels. We are due to have the event at a very plush hotel. I've looked it up actually and it's smack in the middle of Manhattan. Deaf Knee, a few folk from the event company and I are heading out (see, doing it already!) early in order to ensure that all's well. There will be over three hundred attendees at each of three consecutive 'shows', although the Chairman can only attend two with the Deputy Chairman filling in as the understudy for the last event. I don't know the Dep. Chair, Christopher Highlander, at all and we have to brief him next week. Apparently, he's the very opposite of the Chairman and one has to watch one's Ps and Qs.

Arthur

22

From: Arthur Shilling [arthur.shilling@gammondhopes.com]
Sent: 10/06/2011 07.16 AM GMT
To: Steven Charteris [stevencharteris@staracademy.com]
Subject: Sustainability speech and others

Steve

I've had to focus on Mr F over the last week – the sustainability speech and also now one on 'financial impurities in a growth market'. The research on both has been (reasonably) interesting and I've been introduced to a number of in-company specialists, most of whom are senior. The sustainability material is already fairly well-formed and Mr Bose's advice to get ahead of myself was appropriate given my current workload. The material on financial impurities has been more difficult, but once I understood that it was all about 'bad' loans and the current financial sobriety, I found it all very straightforward, although the word 'impurities' won't sit well with Mr F.

My recent sessions with Mr Flattergleich have been interesting. We are doing well with both speeches and we've agreed that he and I will produce detailed notes which we'll gradually reduce so that onstage he'll have simple bullet points with which to work. He wants to walk around the stage and that's fine – I've made a note to advise the production people (a different company from the Forum crew) that they need to light the stage areas accordingly. He also wants a Q&A session after his speech and that, I think, is a good idea because he's excellent at answering questions concisely and precisely. He's also good at admitting that he doesn't know a particular thing and will always promise to come back to the questioner with the right answer – and he does.

Mr Goodenhardt has been asking a great deal of questions about the speeches, but I've kept everything secret – I'm certain that he has it in for Mr F. I've discussed the matter with Mr Bose who has said that I'm doing the right thing by being quiet and saying nothing. He gave me a long, hard look and then went back to tapping a beat on the lift door (since that's where we were). I do seem to spend an inordinate amount of time in lifts – maybe I should write a book about lift behaviour and etiquette.

At one of my script meetings with Mr F, he once again stared off into the mid-distance when we began discussing man's cruelty to man (sustainability). For some reason he wanted a quote from John Steinbeck. I mentioned one from *The Grapes of Wrath* and Mr F became even more involved in his reverie and I knew not where he was or what was going on in his head, so I kept quiet. "Ah," said he eventually, "Ze Gwapes off Rass. It is difficult, Artur, to understand how mush difficulties ze Joad family – and uzzers – had to abenden zare landt und head off into de…" He halted and I said, "Sunset?" "Yes, sunzet," said he. I must point out that, while he was heavily accented, he sounded like a great German sage and I always knew what he was talking about. His voice and timbre demanded attention even if his current presentation style didn't.

We talked a great deal about Steinbeck and *The Battle Hymn of the Republic* from which the book's title comes: "He is trampling out the vintage where the grapes of wrath are stored." "You know, Artur," said Mr F, "De tidle of Shteinbeck's book comes from Ze Beddle Hymn of dee Republic: 'He is trempling…' und so on." He paused. "Faust is good. You know him? Goethe of course also." Before I could answer, he continued: "A story aboud ze mann who zells his zole to ze deffil – here called Mephistopheles – in return for verldly suggszess. He is safed by angels." He paused and then said somewhat sadly I thought, "Mine father was a specialist from Goethe. Und, I am sorry – and, we all sell our zoles one vay and anudder." And so our conversations continued in similar vein. They were a little one-sided, but I like to think that Mr Flattergleich likes me, likes the fact that I can speak German a little and likes the fact that I like his literary bent. He always asks after my efforts at Shakespeare.

Arthur

23

From: Arthur Shilling [arthur.shilling@gammondhopes.com]
Sent: 10/20/2011 05.16 AM GMT
To: Steven Charteris [stevencharteris@staracademy.com]
Subject: More Mr F

Steven

I had spent a good chunk of my recent time getting both of Mr Flattergleich's speeches in tip-top condition and Mr Bose (for one) said that I'd done a good job. The speeches went round the usual offices for reviewing and that led to the usual changes and changing the changes. On this round of 'find the mistake and add a political line or two', Mr Goodenhardt demanded to see the speech drafts and his changes were radical. Mr Bose, on finding this out, told me to sit tight and the next day I had a note from Mr G saying that he was off to America and thought that my drafts were actually fine. He is some hero that Mr B.

The first speech on sustainability went pretty well considering that the speaker before Mr F went on and on and on. At one point, he (an aged professor from a Danish university – a specialist in wind farming, I think) became so excited that he went to point at something on the huge screen, not remembering or knowing that there was a metre gap between the stage and said screen. He quickly discovered that the screen was not hard, but soft – and nearly disappeared down the gap and a drop of some three and a half metres. There was a sharp intake of collective breath from the totally bored audience, suddenly alert to some possible excitement. Then a few titters and the now slightly pale and perspiring academic just tottered about a bit and carried on for another twenty minutes over his allotted time. Mr F was furious because the audience were almost comatose with boredom by now. But, Mr F's speech did pick up the pace and others did complement me on my speech creation prowess even if Mr F has not received five stars for presentation technique or delivery. But, he wasn't bad and his big grin at me on his way out was worth the whole caboodle.

I was not so fortunate, however, later that week, when he came to present his speech on 'communications in a financial downturn'. We decided, or he did, that 'financial impurities in the growth market' was definitely a *nicht nicht* as far as titles went. Anyway, I did my due diligence on research and had good briefing meetings with various in-house specialists.

Jez Staffordhire, Director of IPIDL (and not one who would normally take delight in getting involved with any speeches), decided that he wanted to lend a helping hand with this speech and, in any case, was giving another at the same event. Jez, a very portly gentleman and always short of breath, would waddle along corridors, his jowls bouncing in perfect rhythm against his shiny white shirts, while what was inside the shirts tended to wobble with its own dance routine. Unfortunately, Jez always had a strange smell about him, of what I never could say – something that made him unloved as an elevator companion – and there were terrible occasions when, after a long lunch (of which he took many), he would expel wind from a variety of orifices – loudly and prolonged – accompanied usually by a satisfied smile and an adjustment to his tie.

I don't know why Jez decided to become involved in this speech, but he took it upon himself to point me in various directions as to content, most of which I failed to understand. Jez had something of a nasal twang and whine as he spoke – another factor which didn't really encourage many friendships. "Arfur, go and get last mumf's figures on the rise in profits from our main competitors. And slot those in somewhere. Plus. Plus. Go and get several mumf's worf of figs for EMEA and global profits. That needs to go in. Plus. Plus. When you next run through this speech content with Flattergleich, I want to be there if you please. Lunchtime already is it? Off you toddle then." And similar. Anyway, we rehearsed and prepared, prepared and rehearsed. Jez did not really cut the mustard with Mr F and in fact, my client's patience was thinning at the presence of the large man from IPIDL. Came the day before the event and we had a few disasters all of which ended up being 'my fault'. Two were notably painful.

The production company had set up the stage and backdrop with branding and screens all duly in place. I was treated to a tour backstage where there were neat cables snaking around the floor, held tidily together by yellow tape. Hazard warnings became hazards and technicians were poring over computers, their faces lit with the white and green glow from the screens. Each member of the crew was wearing earphones and there seemed to be some sort of joke doing the rounds. When they saw me, they paused and looked intently at their screens but I noticed that, once I'd passed, the ribaldry began once more.

On stage there was a lectern, but it hadn't been properly fixed to the stage given that its innards and electrics had yet to be completed. All was going pretty well until Jez, getting into his stride with his own speech rehearsal, leaned against said lectern. The lectern wobbled, but he didn't seem to notice because, I suppose, wobbling was part of his daily experience. Suddenly, after more shaking, the lectern (a big thing) fell stage left and along with it the mighty Jez Staffordhsire. There was a crash and a shriek. Nobody moved. Then a producer rushed forward waving her arms and shouting, "Oh my God! My lectern!" Then others rushed around and a cameraman, barely containing his mirth, helped Jez up. His (Jez's) shirt was riding up around his neck and his trousers were about his ankles. His breath came in short bursts. Someone gave him water. He looked around and his eyes fixed on me. "Shilling," he whispered in a dramatic way, "you're in deep troubelle." At that, he limped out of the auditorium, adjusting his clothing as he went and waving off a production assistant who was trying to be of some assistance in hoisting up the fallen trousers.

The second occurrence took place on the same day, but this time with Mr F. I had prepared his notes on cards – all nicely set out and spaced as he likes. Once he started rehearsing, however, things began to go awry. He lost his place, became annoyed with himself then with me, muttering to the world in German. Then the PowerPoint operator lost her place and the wrong images came up, followed by the arm-waving producer flapping around on stage looking at the damaged lectern and dented stage. And to top it all, Mr Goodenhardt had decided to see what was happening. This last was the final straw for Mr F, who took great exception to see the smooth American smiling at the back of the auditorium with his arms folded. Mr F looked at me and said "*Ich bin wirklich unglücklich mit ihnen und ihrem Verhalten.*" ("I am seriously unhappy with you and your behaviour.") For good measure he added in English, "You I am seriously not heppy mit," and walked out. I glanced about for an ally and then, seeing that I had no friends in the room, strode off as if I had somewhere important to go.

I suffer for my art and am probably in deep trouble.

Arthur

24

From: Arthur Shilling [arthur.shilling@gammondhopes.com]
Sent: 10/25/2011 09.16 AM GMT
To: Steven Charteris [stevencharteris@staracademy.com]
Subject: Oh dear, oh dear, oh very dear

Steven

I was virtually ignored for a few days. When he passed me in corridors, Jez just looked straight ahead, stiffened as much as his vast frame would allow and wobbled by without acknowledgement. Khalif Almoun bounced about much as usual (a bit like the child-catcher in the *Chitty Chitty Bang Bang* movie), clicked his fingers, shot people with said fingers and winked – but not at me. Mr Derek Rattles looked hard at me when we passed, but he said nothing. I saw the stupid producer who was more concerned about her wretched grey stage carpet and monstrosity of a lectern than anything else and she just shook her head and said, "Tough luck – we all make mistakes. The lectern's fine by the way."

My landlady, the delicious Victoria Holyhead, was sympathetic and allowed me to mess about with some greasepaint and a stipple sponge which, when applied to self, made me look like a bearded Al Pacino in *Taxi Driver*. I wanted to play with a blood rig (a whole system of tubes which allows a 'wound' to gush blood) that she was preparing for a TV series, but she wouldn't let me and, anyway, that would have done nothing to assuage my gloom.

The next day I was in a meeting chaired by Mr Flattergleich and, while he wasn't as harsh as Jez, he said little that was directed at me. I was totally overlooked during the Q&A time. I sat next to Zalautha Derong during the meeting and at least she bore me no ill will and even offered me some of cheese and onion crisps, although she wouldn't part with any of her cheese and pickle sandwich which she nibbled surreptitiously throughout the meeting much to the annoyance of all – given that the cheese was obviously French and strong with attendant smell to match.

Yours on the sea of desolation

Arthur

25

From: Arthur Shilling [arthur.shilling@gammondhopes.com]
Sent: 10/28/2011 11.16 AM GMT
To: Steven Charteris [stevencharteris@staracademy.com]
Subject: Better

Steven

Normalcy seems to have returned, although nothing has been said. I've tried to apologise to Khalif Almoun since he's my line manager but, every time I tried, he would change the subject and never really listened. I do believe that Miss Smarty Pants producer did find herself at the sharp end of a conversation about something or other from Mr Rattles and Mr Rattles' PA. What I should have said to her when I passed her later that day was "Tough luck. We all make mistakes," but didn't. What I did say was, "Good morning and how are we today?" followed by a Flashman smile. She just looked hard at me and then walked away.

I had to meet with Christopher Highlander, our Deputy Chairman, concerning the New York Executive Forum. I actually discovered from Mrs Sourdough that it's "Sir Christopher to you, young man." In the meeting, Mr Bose was extremely helpful and actually Jez was on good form although we all winced when he said anything. "New York is appaaarently all ready to go," he said, "and has been for a mumf or so and the production people are insistent that we can comfortably get 350 into each event should dat pwoove expedient or necessaaawy." Sir Christopher raised an eyebrow at Jez but otherwise didn't much change from his normal, frowning, serious demeanour. He was crumbling a biscuit (a Swedish oatmeal as I recall) onto his notes, but looking all the time at people around the table as if checking for something on their faces. When he did speak, it was a sharp, metallic screech and therefore it was best when he just nodded or listened. Afterwards I asked Mr Bose what I should do about the Deputy Chairman's opening address and he advised me to change a few parts to suit the American audience and he kindly gave me some pointers as to Sir C's style. He also suggested that I reduce the length a little given the difference in voice between the Chairman and his Deputy. Very subtle is Mr Bose; he gives away little of what he's thinking and less about his private life. I do sometimes still notice him talking animatedly into his mobile phone at coffee time and he also absently drums with pencils on his desk, quietly I must add.

New York is approaching fast and I have no idea whether to take only business attire or some casual clothes as well. Deaf Knee will know, but she's in Hong Kong for some meetings this week. I've made sure that her 30-point list has been thoroughly done and dusted, although I was stuck on point number 26 which read 'Ensure that G or J don't interfere with any of the presentations or the running order.' The trouble with initials is that they could refer to a variety of folk and, in any case, I don't have that much clout to stop anyone doing anything, let alone those with names beginning with a G or a J.

One of my next assignments will be to write, or rather draft, a script for a video programme that the UK Communication Department is making about a number of new training initiatives. IPDL's involved of course. The idea is to produce an internal commercial which will be distributed throughout the offices in the EMEA region. Mr Derek Rattles is managing this project, although the people seen most often are the film director and producer, both of whom seem to be from the planet Zog. "Oh hi Arthur," said Ted, the director person. "If you come unstuck on the script draft then Gargoyle here will bash it into shape, OK? We're not sure whether we're going anamorphic yet, but that shouldn't worry you. And we might try some audio bridging, but we can talk about that later too. Cool?" Meanwhile, Gargoyle the producer says little, but writes many a scribble into his red Moleskin notebook. Gargoyle of course isn't his name but it sounded like that. The idea for the video was his apparently and it will feature Mr Rattles and someone from Risk who apparently is very good as a frontman and presenter. Ted says that "They don't want too much dialogue and most of the footage will be slow-mo coverage of the training materials and 'sexy' page turns of the training manuals." Sounds very dull. I did try and suggest an alternative and so did Mr Bose although neither idea was exactly *Gone With the Wind* or maybe that's exactly what they were. Gargoyle is deeply disturbing.

I also have to play an active part in a committee set up to discuss and debate the company's strategy on social media. Sounds interesting. We'll see. Am still feeling below par and greatly unloved, but Mr Bose told me to snap out of it and get on.

Best

Arthur

26

From: Arthur Shilling [arthur.shilling@gammondhopes.com]
Sent: 11/02/2011 11.16 PM GMT
To: Steven Charteris [stevencharteris@staracademy.com]
Subject: Social media

Steven

The social media meetings have been intensely interesting. Facebook is apparently on the wane, allowing (as someone in the meeting said – I think it was Porteous Generafrey from Argentina) "online networking tools to proliferate". I've been asked to prepare a presentation for the next meeting on the networking tools that will proliferate. More homework.

Midsummer Night's Dream is rehearsing well. The lisper is in it, as are most of the *Hamlet* players. My Bottom is holding up and, while I lust after Titania, I am behaving myself – which is more than might be said about a Jeremy Tyndale from Group Training who speaks with such a plum in his mouth that he makes a mockery of his role as Peter Quince. He takes his role as a carpenter a bit far as the nominal leader of the craftsmen's attempt to put on a play for Theseus' marriage celebration. Ha, listen to me telling you! Well, you know when Quince is meant to be shoved aside by the abundantly confident Bottom? Jeremy keeps forgetting his part and shoves back, thereby causing me multiple bruises and now a chipped tooth. During the craftsmen's play, when Quince plays the Prologue, Jeremy shouts and therefore ruins all that has gone before. I shall have a word with our esteemed but strange producer, old Nookles. Thank goodness my chum Graham Graveling is a fairy.

Now, off to prep my 'online networking tools presentation'. And to pack for NY, NY!

Best as ever

Arthur

P.S. Please tell your good lady wife that I saw her on TV last night when she was bundled into the police car. Very impressive language!

27

From: Arthur Shilling [arthur.shilling@gammondhopes.com]
Sent: 11/05/2011 19.16 PM GMT
To: Steven Charteris [stevencharteris@staracademy.com]
Subject: Mostly apologies

Professor Charteris

Sir, I do so humbly apologise for causing you so much grief re my silly comment about your wife's re-arrest. I quite understand why you called so late and equally I understand your undisguised fury, although your threats might have been thought through a little. Who knows who was listening? These days, what with hacking and goodness knows what... No, I don't want to compound my felony. Please accept my apologies once more and I promise that there'll be no mention of anything like that again. I do really hope that we may continue our dialogue. I find it really helpful.

Well, all packed and ready for the off! New York tomorrow. I shall miss two rehearsals of *The Dream*, but I'm not in every scene and, anyway, I feel that I know my part (and almost everyone else's really) so, while I might be missed, all should be well. Mrs Sourdough wanted to know what I was up to of an evening and I told her at length about the overconfident weaver chosen to play Pyramus in the craftsmen's play for Theseus' marriage celebration and how my Bottom is full of advice and self-confidence but frequently makes silly mistakes and misuses language. She looked slightly aghast and it didn't much help when I got into my stride about Bottom's simultaneous nonchalance about the beautiful Titania's sudden love for him and unawareness of the fact that Puck has transformed his head into that of an ass. She just said, "I see, Mr Shilling. I see. Well I can make out Deidre Davenport from Accounts over there wanting to go for a coffee or some such thing, so I'll leave you to it. You and your bottom." I suspect that Shakespeare is not her strong suit. Mr Bose, on the other hand, said apropos of not much, that he'd played Peaseblossom, Cobweb, Mote and Mustardseed – in the same production at school when he was seven. I didn't explore that one because I was so very gobsmacked that he'd told me anything about his background. The very thought of a young Mr Bose prancing about in surgical tights and gossamer and playing numerous fairies all at once just made me boggle-eyed for a while.

Best (and, once again, I do apologise for the irritation caused to you and Mrs C. I trust that the pot plant helped.)

Arthur

28

From: Arthur Shilling [arthur.shilling@gammondhopes.com]
Sent: 11/07/2011 13.16 PM EST
To: Steven Charteris [stevencharteris@staracademy.com]
Subject: Noo York!

Professor Charteris

We're here. I shall have to be moderately brief because there is a mass of stuff to do. Deaf Knee has been here for three days already and Mr Goodenhardt is all over everything like a rash as is Mr Flattergleich, neither of whom have yet fully forgiven me for what they think was my mistake with the falling lectern and the fact that I'm not Jenny Barstiff, etc.

Mr Goodenhardt is actually being moderately pleasant in fits and starts – primarily because he wants info on the delectable Jenny, who remains on a yellow card as far as the department is concerned.

I have already spent three long hours going through Deaf Knee's checklist. She calls it something else but the lawyers say that I can't repeat it. We've met the hotel's banqueting and event managers, both of whom have perfect teeth and hair. There's a light on but the eyes are slightly dimmed. Tired I think. Or drugs. Then we met four of the speakers who are here already and each of whom

I know from the London show. I'm one of the team now because they all shook my hand, grinned and welcomed me to the capital of the free world. Tomorrow we have full-blown rehearsals and the Deputy Chairman's arriving so everyone's getting a bit nervy about that.

On the plane (business class – great films and great service!) I produced the first draft of my presentation on social media and the like. Not bad but I want to send it to Mr Bose before forwarding it to anyone else. Actually, I think I'm on my own with this one, but Mr B is a very good wicket keeper. Let me try some of it on you. Or at least some of the big points:

- I'll introduce the six different types of social media:
  collaborative projects (like Wikipedia), blogs and microblogs
  (such as Twitter), content communities (YouTube being
  a good example), social networking sites (like Facebook),
  virtual game worlds (like World of Warcraft) and virtual
  social worlds (like Second Life). Technologies include blogs,
  picture-sharing, email, instant messaging, music-sharing,
  crowdsourcing and voice-over IP amongst others. Many
  of these social media services can be integrated via social
  network aggregation platforms. Not bad so far, eh?

- **Facebook:** The good points – easy to sign up, clean design,
  supports personal and brand/interest pages. Excellent for
  photo sharing and event management. Bad points – it's
  too big and that's led to diversification and corporate
  meddling. Less people are signing up, maybe people find the
  whole thing too intrusive. Microsoft bought Skype in 2011 for
  £5.4bn and the alliance of Microsoft, Skype and Facebook is a
  powerful trinity. I like that, don't you: a powerful trinity?

- **Twitter**: Founded in 2006, 300m plus registered users and 200m tweets sent every day! This is a short, sharp blogging-style service with messages limited to 140 characters – a global texting device really. The good points: it's quick and easy to use and more open than Facebook – mainly used as a news gathering and live blog tool plus it can focus quickly on crowd activism. Twitter users can follow anyone who chooses to make their tweets public. Bad things: there's now a lot of message babble.

- **Google+**: Founded in 2011 and heading for 20m users. This is Google's battle with Facebook. Google is moving away from being only a search engine supplier and now seeks to build *the* hub for socialising and content-sharing. What's good about it? Google+ uses separate friend networks, instantly solving the Facebook worry over sharing dubious YouTube videos with a singular friend list that includes your boss or former university professor! Some say that it's more or less the same as Facebook under a different brand name. But Google has such a long reach that Facebook will struggle to beat it. Facebook has the scale, but Google+ has the connectivity. (Mr Bose liked that.)

- **Tumblr**: Founded in 2007 with 400m page views a day. This is all about blogging. The key is content rather than how famous you are. It's a bit like a digital scrapbook – a place to show off creative work, photography and art. It's popular and people see it as a place to share ideas. Not least once Lady Gaga joined up!

- **LinkedIn**: Founded in 2003 and has over 100m users. This is a business-based networking tool. It used to be regarded as a place to post a CV, but it's now *the* place to be if you've had an employment setback. LinkedIn is great at introducing users to people they don't know or used to know but have lost track of. It establishes introductions. The weak thing about it is that it has little charisma and is a bit dry.

- **Foursquare**: Founded in 2009 with 10m registered users and designed for mobile phones. Users earn points for checking in and marking points of interest. It turns the mundane business of reality into a game. The more you check in to a particular place, store or business, the greater the number of points you gain. It's limited and people seem to be excited to start with, then get bored.

- **Quora**: Founded in 2009 with around 1.5m registered users. This is a bit like Wikipedia and is a knowledge-based, interactive tool. It can feel a little like an online debating site, but it also seems a tad geeky and technical for a wide audience.

And there's more, but I don't want to bore you. These are just notes but I want to present using very simple bullet points. Anyway, I'd best be off. Have to watch the lighting being plotted. And then we'll go through the walk-in, walk-out music and also see that everything's OK for the event facilitator – who, this time, is a *very* big American star from primetime TV. I'm not allowed to mention his name.

For now, *ciao bambino*, as they say in these here parts. Actually they say 'ged ouda here', smile and thump you in the shoulder.

Arthur

29

From: Arthur Shilling [arthur.shilling@gammondhopes.com]
Sent: 11/09/2011 16.16 PM EST
To: Steven Charteris [stevencharteris@staracademy.com]
Subject: Beaten to a pulp

Steven

The event was a success by all accounts. I missed most of it, having had a small altercation with the police the night before last. I had been asked to check who came into rehearsals and, on pain of death, not to let anyone in who wasn't on my clipboard list. This was on the instruction of the Deputy Chairman's office, so nobody was going to argue, least of all me. Trouble was I had to check speaker support (PowerPoint), as well as greet speakers and make sure that someone was looking after coffee and 'soda requirements' for anyone at a higher level than me. I also had to generally leap to attention each time Deaf Knee asked for something or exclaimed with horror because something wasn't quite right. And all that on top of the production people talking too fast at me and saying 'youse' a great deal. If I said 'pardon' once I said it a gazillion times and then they would say "pardon me" and "I didn't get that" and "Hey Art, wog wan man?" The last apparently means "what's up?" or "how are you doing today my fine fellow?" or "what's going on?". Occasionally I was bombarded with, "I'm from Brooknam. You?" And I just nodded inanely, probably with drool dribbling down my chin to complete the idiot look. Apparently 'Brooknam' is a combination of Brooklyn and Vietnam, given the violent nature of the NY district.

Anyway, all was going reasonably well during rehearsals, apart from our Deputy Chairman speaking like a rusty hinge and wandering about all over the stage. The event producer was having fun with him (not) and the two clearly were getting on rather badly – much to the consternation of and interference by Sir C's acolytes, assistants and general factotums.

Suddenly the auditorium's double doors swung open and in walked a huge man wearing trainers (sneakers here), jeans and a sweatshirt bearing the Yankees symbol. He was chewing gum and, at the same time, talking loudly. I spun round and went "shhhhhh" as did some of the general populous but then, seeing his attire, I thought that this man and his two thug attendees were miscreants who'd come into the wrong place. I went up to the big chap and said "Sorry, this is a private event and we're rehearsing. Would you mind leaving?" The man stopped talking and also ceased chewing. The two sidekicks looked me up and down and the back of my neck went cold. The big man said, "You axing me ter leave?" He turned to his pals and continued jerking a big thumb in my direction, "This lamestain wants fer me to leave! Haw haw!" Now to me, he said, "I tink you de one who gotta be bounced pal." He then pushed me in the chest. Well I'm not a brave chap, really not, but that annoyed me and I pushed him back. Suddenly I was on the floor pinned down by the two heavies and being pummelled everywhere. In the meantime, Mr Big was striding towards the stage and the Deputy Chairman where everyone was smiles and handshakes. It turns out that this rude gent is actually Josh Stonewall, General Manager, Retail Banking here on the east coast of the United States.

Anyway, I was hauled off to the onsite police depot for questioning and alleged assault. Nobody came to my aid apart from Mr Flattergleich who (eventually) vouched for me. However, I was so bruised and battered that I had to take to my bed and then overslept the first morning of the event – much to the dismay (irritation) of Dephne and, well, everyone really. When I did show my face, black and blue as it was (a treat for my landlady's study by the by), everyone avoided me. That is until Mr Big, looking every bit the professional footballer he used to be – but now sporting a smart suit – saw me and strode over, pushing a wide variety of delegates out of the way. "Ardy, Ardy," he bellowed. "No hard feelin's huh?" He grabbed my right hand and shook it, then clasped me to his ample bosom. "Lookit, sorry boud lass nide. Notchyourfauld. All mine. Youse juss doin' yer job, ride?" I nodded bleakly. "Lookit. If you get some R&R here in Noo Yorg Siddy, den led me know and it'd be my grade honour to entertain youse! K?" Again, I nodded bleakly and felt much like crying, truth be told. He pushed his face close to mine and said, "You're OK son. OK. And I am sorry boud wad happinnd," and then was gone, leaving behind the scent of some very expensive aftershave. Well, that opened the floodgates and I wept briefly (wish I could do that on stage) and then suddenly everyone who knew me – and who'd seen the chat – rushed over and more or less asked me to be their best friend for ever and ever, such is the influence of Josh Stonewall (aptly named methinks).

Bruised

Arthur

30

From: Arthur Shilling [arthur.shilling@gammondhopes.com]
Sent: 11/12/2011 23.16 PM GMT
To: Steven Charteris [stevencharteris@staracademy.com]
Subject: Back home

Well, Steven,

I'm back in the old UK and not a little relieved actually. I did receive an email from the Deputy Chairman thanking me for my hard work and contribution and I also received a very kind note from the office of Josh Stonewall. I never did manage the R&R offer but, bless him, the note did say that the offer was open for the next time I was in NY. International friends hey? Mr Bose, who does not stand on ceremony, looked coolly at my bruises (which my landlady had offered to make disappear, but I quite liked being able to tell tales of terrible New York beatings at the hands of *West Side Story*-like Jets) and made some welcome corrections to my presentation on social media which I gave today. While it wasn't necessarily an Obama keynote, several colleagues did say that it was good stuff. Khalif Almoun, my manager, was actually in the room for once and stayed the whole time, a first for me. He winked at me on the way out and shot me with his fingers so I guess (see what the USA does?) I'm back in his good books.

The bank is in the process of buying a number of smaller institutions at the moment and I have to assist the PR department in the form of Gloria Mishmash.

It was good to get back to my *Midsummer Night's Dream* rehearsals, although, seemingly, I hadn't been much missed. My landlady, Victoria Holyhead, wanted to photograph my bruises. I wonder if I should have asked for money?

Best

Arthur

>

From: Steven Charteris [stevencharteris@staracademy.com]
Sent: 11/15/2011 09.16 AM GMT
To: Arthur Shilling [arthur.shilling@gammondhopes.com]
Subject: Refer to our friend, Shakespeare, for solace

"The quality of mercy is not strain'd,
It droppeth as the gentle rain from heaven
Upon the place beneath. It is twice blest:
It blesseth him that gives and him that takes."

Portia: *Merchant of Venice* (IV, i)

Arthur

I have to say that I very nearly ended our correspondence after your tasteless remark about Mrs Charteris and her current difficulties. Her discomfort has been considerable and the issue with the police inspector was totally innocent. I would be grateful in due course for a modest sum to be paid into Mrs C's charity, *Displaced Dolphins*. In your own time of course. Next week would suit.

Now then, let bygones be bygones and let us also express the quality of mercy. My, what a busy and complex time you've been having of things! I am slightly troubled because I sense a smidgen of immodesty and a holier-than-thou attitude creeping into your psyche. It must go! You are a junior on the lowest rung of corporate and executive life. You must observe and learn, do your best and apply your ready intelligence. It isn't your place to be judgmental. People will not tolerate it and cynicism has no real place. Think on.

People

- You are surrounded by a variety of personalities and many are trying to outdo the next – or so it seems. People play games and some folk will always try and get one step ahead of the competition. Such is life.

- Mr Flattergleich sounds like a decent man who is trying hard to improve his presentation skills. His accent will improve with your help and I must say that I am very impressed at the dialogue that you and he share.

- Mr Bose is a case of still waters running deep and it's fantastic that he remains something of a guiding light and mentor to you. The fact that he keeps himself to himself and beats a rhythm on his desk from time to time is of no matter.

Presentations

- Mr F's sustainability speech wasn't an easy one by the sounds of it, but you did all the right things: research, drafts, taking advice, bullet points, refining and refining again. You are beginning to know your 'client' and that must help enormously in your speech-writing. The scenario you paint of the Danish professor almost falling down the rear of the stage area is entertaining although serious as well; of course it is incumbent on the event producer or someone in charge to make all speakers aware of the dangers onstage. Maybe in future you should ensure that the producer has remembered to inform all contributors about stage health and safety.

- The fact that Mr Flattergleich became irritated and then angry with you because he lost his place isn't really your fault, although there may have been something in how you set out his notes and bullet points that confused him. Given that you were close to the speech (and the deliverer), you could have stepped in and called a halt – thereby allowing everyone to sort themselves out. That's what rehearsals are for. Or, better still, a quiet word with the producer at the beginning of rehearsals would have paid dividends. You might then have mentioned Mr F's style of presentation and the possible difficulties that might have arisen.

- The position in which you found yourself concerning Mr Staffordshire was most unfortunate and I can't see that the collapse of the lectern followed by his good self was anything to do with you. Perhaps the producer should have advised him and others accordingly that the lectern was not yet fixed. Also, I imagine Mr S felt very embarrassed at his loss of face (and indeed much of his clothing). The fact that he has an unfortunate speaking voice and way of pronouncing words doesn't mean that he shouldn't be afforded respect. I feel that you could have faced up to the problem with Mr S rather than let the matter go. That would have allowed him to vent his spleen and you would have made your case as to being reasonably faultless. There the matter would (or should) have rested.

- Zalautha Derong, she who consumes cheese and onion crisps with cheese and pickle sandwiches, seems odd but I can't believe that she does little or nothing. If she is a fluent French speaker, then this may be one of the skills for which she is employed. However, in a large corporation, the levels of hard work vary but, in the end, those who are slack do tend to get found out.

- Your line manager, Khalif Almoun, sounds like a real character and, again, I can't believe the picture you paint of someone who does little.

- It seems to me as if you did the right things in your dealings with your Deputy Chairman. Managing relationships with very senior executives is always tough for junior staff and the process can be a bit daunting. Watch and listen rather than say things you would later regret. And well done for writing and managing Sir Christopher's NY opening address.

Video programmes – some thoughts

- Making corporate video programmes is a specialist skill. The first thing to do is decide exactly what your main message will be. What is the most important thing that viewers should be thinking when watching the video for the first time? If the purpose of the programme is to stimulate discussion, what do you want viewers to be talking about? Any video should have one main message. All the examples given, and all subsequent messages in the video, should support and reinforce this main message or proposition.

- Be clear about the video's purpose. Work out who is going to see it and where it's going to be seen. Keep the purpose narrow and defined. Many companies try to take a Swiss army knife approach to commissioning a video or film. They want it for internal orientation and communications. They also want to show it at exhibitions and they want sales people to use it. They might also want it to be downloaded – and so on. Trying to make one programme fit a myriad of purposes will diminish the impact of the main message.

- Videos aren't cheap to produce, so a good question to posit is: do we really need a video at all? Videos work best when they *show* something – there are many corporate videos that do the job of a brochure, but less well. A video should show the viewer action relevant to your proposition. If your message could just as easily be put across using text and graphics or simple animation, or a brochure, web page or (heavens preserve us) a PowerPoint presentation, well then a video isn't the right solution.

- How is your video going to fit in with other materials such as a web page, brochure, catalogue or training materials, and how is it going to be distributed – DVD perhaps, or video streaming from a website?

- Work out how much you can afford to spend and be realistic. Asking a production company how much a video will cost to make is like asking the length of a piece of string. It's much better to decide on a budget and then let your supplier tell you what they can do for the price. The same goes for time constraints. The more time there is to prepare (within reason), the better the quality of the finished item. Usually. Also be prepared for a good agency to challenge the brief. You *may* get a better result by discussing what you think you need linked to what experts may believe you really need.

Arthur, I do realise that the decisions I mention here won't be yours to make (yet), but they're tips for the future.

- When it comes to writing a video script, you need some guidance from the production company, a corporate film writer or colleagues who've done this kind of thing before. A training (or indeed any) programme must open in an engaging way and the flow of information must be smooth and absorbing. Not a second is lost, not a moment wasted. Think of a brilliant TV commercial: a clear proposition and an invitation to buy in 30 seconds (at most).

- Unproven assumptions, too much controversy, wooden actors, unbelievable scenes or claims and a dreadful and unrealistic script can all stop the flow of communication in a corporate video.

- You need to organise your script and the flow of information so that, at every stage, viewers will understand everything they see, even if they don't always agree with it. Anything that is risible or unbelievable will destroy the flow.

Social media revisited
- Social media vehicles allow for instantaneous dissemination of not just news, but images, audio, video and other multimedia content as well. And because releases geared toward social media outlets contain only key highlights, pertinent facts and hyperlinks to related statistics and

quotes, the information they contain can be immediately picked up and posted by bloggers and online journalists.

- Social media also provides more widespread coverage, enabling breaking news to reach a much larger and broader reader base than standard media outlets alone. While magazine readership and the number of available print publications continue to decline, I'm told by our Modern Media Fellow, Pete (never Peter!) Iceland, that the number of consumers using the Internet to access and share information continues to rise sharply.

- Social media, and blogs in particular, can be a highly useful tool for enhancing both awareness and image. Blogging can help 'spread the word' about a company to more people, dramatically increasing brand recognition and awareness.

- Additionally, social media can enable executives to gather insight, input and feedback directly from their target audience and use that intelligence for more effective reputation management.

- Many social media techniques – such as frequent use of key phrases, title tags, ticker symbols and links to blogs and other relevant Web content – can dramatically improve search engine rankings.

- Whenever I am asked to join a meeting to explain digital and social media (and its only because nobody else in the English Department can), I find it easy to do. This is mostly because Mrs C is a blogger, a Twitterholic and a Facebook fanatic, none of which helps her case of course.

America

- You didn't really get a chance to explore that great country. And it is great. Many people rubbish it and its people and that's become a sport. There have been many a dinner party where I have been the only or one of the very few to support American presidents past and present, culture, poetry, food, beverages, history, music, musicals and films.

- Your experience was obviously limited (and a little painful) so I take it you didn't even get much of a chance to explore what New York has to offer. Go back one day.

Catch you later, as they said in *Starsky and Hutch* – circa 1975 or 76. I always identified with the dark haired one. Starsky I think. Or possibly Hutch.

Steven

Chapter Four

"Some Cupid kills with arrows, some with traps."

Hero: *Much Ado About Nothing* (III, i)

31

From: Arthur Shilling [arthur.shilling@gammondhopes.com]
Sent: 11/20/2011 08.16 AM GMT
To: Steven Charteris [stevencharteris@staracademy.com]
Subject: I'm in love

Steven

As ever, thank you very much for your kind comments.

Suddenly all hell's broken loose with the PR activity concerning the purchase of the two small but important banks. I'm in charge of communicating what's going on to other departments. The fearsome Gloria Mishmash, she of uncertain years, is very much in charge – of me.

Gloria gave me a lecture on day one, "Whether you think there's a better alternative or you'd rather receive PR pitches by Twitter, press releases are still a popular format for public relations and communications teams when contacting journalists – particularly concerning financial matters. I have simple rules. Produce accurate information and send it only to the correct people." She is a tiny woman, but dapper, unsmiling and frightening.

Gloria's next-in-command is the most beautiful girl I've ever met. When I was introduced to the PR team, I locked eyes with hers for a nanosecond and am most definitely in love. Her name is Chloe something and she is the main conduit between the bank and the financial press. My job is to produce draft copy for releases that she will check before they go into my department and then to the length and breadth of the bank. Jez Staffordshire, who is still a little arch with me, is meant to be providing departmental support.

Chloe explained how she wanted me to operate – basically to take source information from her and her colleagues and to draft releases for internal use. I listened to half of what she was saying. I am now totally torn between the woman who's playing Titania and Chloe. Both make me go slightly wobbly at the knee.

Mr Bose very kindly drifted over to my new temporary department to see how I was faring. People in PR know him and smile or wave. His responses are always limited to tight smiles or a nod of the head. I was really pleased when he came right to my desk and asked if I was OK and if I was comfortable with what I had to do. Then he drifted off again playing a neat beat on the filing cabinets as he left. There is something definitely *Dark Side of the Moon* about him. I was particularly pleased at his visit for one reason alone. Chloe looked at me with fresh appraisal.

Best

Arthur

32

From: Arthur Shilling [arthur.shilling@gammondhopes.com]
Sent: 11/27/2011 05.16 AM GMT
To: Steven Charteris [stevencharteris@staracademy.com]
Subject: Several

Steven

I now have three current roles: the PR male equivalent of a doyenne for internal information concerning the purchase of the two banks, speechwriter extraordinaire for Mr Flattergleich and video programme scriptwriter supreme. Yes, I know. Modesty.

The internal press releases seem to be going well. Chloe is a hard task mistress and is so busy that flirtation is out of the question, although I do find the odd moment when I can gaze as she flicks a few strands of blonde hair away from her gorgeous face. The new speech for Mr F is on the subject of 'the importance of communications when times are tough' – pretty straightforward I think. The video script, on the other hand, is a disaster. Every time I write something, the wretched producer and director have to see it and they just email back that what I've written is nonsense or rubbish. They have the gall to copy almost everyone in the department and also most of the advertising agency and production company as well. I had a word with the producer and said, "Look, tell me what style you're after and I'll do my best. Or better still, you write a little and show me what's what." He just looked at me and said, "Doesn't work like that Arthur." I've tried to seek help but nobody seems to know what to suggest.

Chloe has just come back from her lunch so I'd better sign off. I've tried hard to practice nonchalance but it doesn't seem to work. People tend to ask me if I'm feeling unwell.

Yours aye,

Arthur

33

From: Arthur Shilling [arthur.shilling@gammondhopes.com]
Sent: 12/01/2011 04.16 AM GMT
To: Steven Charteris [stevencharteris@staracademy.com]
Subject: Video script sorted

Steven

Hurrah and hooray. The department notables were so fed up with being copied on emails from the producer or director about my inability to deliver a proper script that they've insisted that a real scriptwriter be employed. There were, according to Jenny Barstiff (who's still around), raised voices and some red faces, but a professional writer was duly employed and I met him yesterday. He's really nice, quite quiet and (lucky him) wears jeans and a t-shirt with a bright red jacket. He has long, greying hair and I can well imagine him nodding with gratitude as a BAFTA or even an Oscar is handed over to tumultuous applause. Apparently, he's written a great deal for television – mostly murder mystery plays and whodunnits, plus some children's books – adventures and horror for young teens. He says he has a film option being considered at the moment. His name is David Galsworthy (no relation apparently) and I like him. More to the point, he seems to like me and listened very carefully when our in-house team gave him the brief (verbal and written – the latter was a labour of love produced by yours truly at midnight). He asked detailed and intelligent questions, understood what we were on about and relayed some of the producer's views which the meeting debated, absorbed and (I'm pleased to say) chucked out mercilessly. Revenge is a dish etc. Must fly.

Arthur

34

From: Arthur Shilling [arthur.shilling@gammondhopes.com]
Sent: 12/04/2011 07.16 AM GMT
To: Steven Charteris [stevencharteris@staracademy.com]
Subject: Press releases!

Steven

My press release work seems to be reasonably well-received and even my boss, Khalif Almoun, came to visit. He spent most of the time perched on Chloe's desk, one buttock stretching his already tight suit trousers (to the point of eye-watering pain in a lesser man). Once he had distinctly failed to make more than his usual jolly impression on the delectable Chloe, he shrugged and looked around, his eyes eventually alighting upon me. He smiled, pointed and snapped his fingers. Jumping up, he leapt over, gave one of my shoulders a quick pat and was gone.

Chloe has copyedited a few of my releases and initially I was offended, but all of her suggestions have been really helpful. Mr

Bose says that I should use straightforward language. I have, he avers, a tendency to use larger, complex words and phrases when the simple will do. He gave me a huge list that has proved to be very useful and has put me in Chloe's good books. He also spent a couple of hours showing me how to edit complicated material to become plain English.

Must rush. Again. Best to you and Mrs C. How *is* she?

Arthur

35

From: Arthur Shilling [arthur.shilling@gammondhopes.com]
Sent: 12/07/2011 04.16 AM GMT
To: Steven Charteris [stevencharteris@staracademy.com]
Subject: Rehearsals

Steven

Well, Chloe has only asked if she can come and see *Midsummer Night's Dream*! Oh my goodness. Should I have mentioned the play at all? Was that a terrible mistake? What if she thinks my Bottom is stupid and what if she's a *real* theatre buff? By the way, will you be able to come down and see this one? Do try. I know that it's always difficult what with Mrs C and all. But do try and then you can meet some of my colleagues. We might even be able to go for a drink or you could come to the cast party after the last night.

Anyway, the internal communications about the company's purchases are progressing nicely, although I am in danger of repeating epithets. Chloe is an exacting boss and quickly returns anything that she regards as repetitive or dull. I think that I 'get' press releases now although I am being careful, as you suggested, not to be too cocky. Deidre Sissons (also on loan from my department) is not faring that well. Makes terrible grammatical mistakes and keeps forgetting 'i' before 'e' except after 'c' and similar rules.

I've been asked to read through the new corporate training video script and it's really good. Like it. Wish I could write like him.

Arthur

36

From: Arthur Shilling [arthur.shilling@gammondhopes.com]
Sent: 12/10/2011 15.16 PM GMT
To: Steven Charteris [stevencharteris@staracademy.com]
Subject: Jez

Steven

Jez Staffordshire called me in for a meeting and he seems to have more or less forgiven me for my alleged transgressions. I know this because he joked to the rest of the meeting, none of whom I knew: "Ah, here's Arfur, he who puts hunsuspecting souls in dire peril on stage. Do not lean against any stage furnishing in his presence. You hev been warn… ed!" I suspect that something has happened to his front teeth because they seem crooked. I do hope that it wasn't the stage tumble that did that. But he was smiling – albeit weakly. Apparently, there have been a few blockages to the communications concerning the bank purchase deal and Sir

Christopher is hopping mad. Big Jez told us that first we had to identify the barrier. "If you can figure out what the problem is," he said, "you'll have a heasier time figurin' out how to hovercome hit." I sighed inwardly.

Jez told us to ask questions and listen to the replies with an open mind. He also said that woe betide anyone if he, Jez, got yelled at again by someone in the Deputy Chairman's office. Then he sighed theatrically and bowed his head as if in deep thought. Or indigestion. We left Jez's office not 100% clear what we had to do.

Arthur

37

From: Arthur Shilling [arthur.shilling@gammondhopes.com]
Sent: 12/14/2011 15.16 PM GMT
To: Steven Charteris [stevencharteris@staracademy.com]
Subject: Words

Steven

I fear that I am about to leave the gorgeous Chloe and rejoin the Almoun, Bose and Sourdough set. Ah well. Enjoyable while it lasted. Chloe thanked me for my hard work and contribution. She actually shook my hand, but there was no flicker of 'what might you be doing after work this evening?' in her eyes. Back to Titania I think.

I attended a presentation given by a visiting communications expert from the University of Galawash, Australia. This gentleman is ex-Oxford and has made a living out of telling companies how to use less words in their communications. I was a bit cynical but Professor Cobhandler's sheer warmth and knowledge was actually contagious. His material was simple but effective, even though he began his session with "G'day". And finished it with "G'day". This kind of thing:

Wordy: After booking a ticket to Edinburgh from a travel agent, I packed my bags and arranged for a taxi to the airport. Once there, I checked in, went through security and was ready to board. But problems beyond my control led to a three-hour delay before takeoff. (47 words)
Concise: My flight to Edinburgh was delayed for three hours. (9 words)

Best to you and, of course, g'day.

Arthur

38

From: Arthur Shilling [arthur.shilling@gammondhopes.com]
Sent: 12/17/2011 22.16 PM GMT
To: Steven Charteris [stevencharteris@staracademy.com]
Subject: Quotes in speeches

Steven

I'm focussing now on Mr F's next speech. He would like to emphasise some of his key points with a number of careful quotes. I've been doing some research and have found excellent examples.

Mr F's speech comes just before coffee and I've found this from the wonderful American preacher, Henry Ward Beecher (*Eyes and Ears*), whose sister wrote *Uncle Tom's Cabin*:

> "A cup of coffee – real coffee – home-browned, home-ground, home-made, that comes to you dark as a hazel-eye, but changes to a golden bronze as you temper it with cream that never cheated, but was real cream from its birth, thick, tenderly yellow, perfectly sweet, neither lumpy nor frothing on the Java: such a coffee is a match for twenty blue devils, and will exorcise them all."

When Mr F discusses the power of communication, I've found this from Gustave Flaubert's *Madame Bovary*:

> "The human language is like a cracked kettle on which we beat out a tune for a dancing bear, when we hope with our music to move the stars."

Towards the end of his speech, Mr F wants to make a point about power and I've found this from JFK's address to Amherst College in 1963:

> "When power leads man toward arrogance, poetry reminds him of his limitations. When power narrows the areas of man's concern, poetry reminds him of the richness and diversity of his existence. When power corrupts, poetry cleanses, for art establishes the basic human truths which must serve as the touchstone of our judgment."

Mr F is impressed as is Mr Bose. Jez less so, but then he chooses not to like much in the way of quotations. Before you say anything, his view is just as valid and, of course, not all speeches need quotes.

Best

Arthur

39

From: Arthur Shilling [arthur.shilling@gammondhopes.com]
Sent: 12/20/2011 18.16 PM GMT
To: Steven Charteris [stevencharteris@staracademy.com]
Subject: Spelling

Steven

The Christmas season is full on and all the big high street shops have dreadful muzak: the same carols over and over again. Grinning Santas affront one on the Underground and when I heard a little girl ask of her mother "Why are there so many Santa Clauses?" I nearly barked something very rude. My landlady, Victoria Holyhead, is very busy with parties where they require extraordinary makeup. This evening she was airbrushing a New York police costume onto a naked young lady! I tried to get an invitation.

Presents are always a problem. Oh, please do thank Mrs C for her early gift (which I had to open) of slightly melted chocolate chess pieces. The postman wasn't pleased. I know your good lady meant well though and a note to her will follow.

Big argument with the powers that be. I was given a document written by my boss, Khalif Almoun, and he'd asked me to knock it into shape for a Management Board paper. Unfortunately, I totally forgot and the paper went in unedited. He was furious, not least because everyone at the meeting found it and him risible. The shame of it! I apologised and grovelled. All Mr Almoun said was, "You are on the pathway out of this gig buddy boy! I hear a trumpet voluntary." I didn't tell him that I thought he might have meant *The Last Post*. Everyone in the department had obviously heard what had happened since nobody would look in my direction and people were seemingly sniggering behind desks and hands. Mr Bose was abroad and Mrs Sourdough just sighed, shook her head in sorrow and muttered at the whole thing being terrible or "some such thing".

I did take the passage and correct it as follows but Mr Almoun was not to be appeased:

'What is climate change?' Mr Almoun's version:

'Climate change is considered by many to be the worlds most important environmental problem which has far reaching impacts on society and the worlds economy human activity over the last 150 years is believed to have caused a significant acceleration in the rate of change of our climate. The following human activities all release Greenhouse Gasses into the atmosfere, burning of fossil fuel such as oil coal gas to produce energy and fuel for transport as well as destroying forests and intensive farming. Greenhouse Gasses trap heats from the sun causing 'global warming' and changing weather conditions across the globe. International scientific opinion marshalled by the Intergovernmental Panel on Climate Change (the IPPC but check this) is responsible for reporting on the global impact of changes to the climate and advising governments on the steps needed to both adapt to climate change and to mitigate its future impact. The three key international, european and national Policies to tackle climates change are the kyoto protocol (2005); EU energy policy (2007 check this); and the draft Climate Change Bill (2007). Ennuf. Arthur sort this for tomoorw plse.'

'What is climate change?' Mr Arthur Shilling's humble version:

'Climate change is considered by many to be the world's most important environmental problem. It has far-reaching impacts on society and the world's economy. Human activity over the last 150 years is believed to have caused a significant acceleration in the rate of change of our climate. The following activities all release greenhouse gases into the atmosphere:

- burning fossil fuels, such as oil, coal and gas, to produce energy and fuel for transport
- destroying forests
- intensive farming

Greenhouse gases trap heat from the sun, causing 'global warming' and changing weather conditions across the globe. International scientific opinion is marshalled by the Intergovernmental Panel on Climate Change (IPPC). It is responsible for reporting on the global impact of changes to the climate and advising governments on the steps needed both to adapt to climate change and to mitigate its future impact. From the UK perspective, there are three key international, European and national policies to tackle climate change:

- Kyoto Protocol (2005)
- EU energy policy (2007)
- draft Climate Change Bill (2007)'

The play begins in a few days and I don't think we're ready. I'm sorry that you won't be able to make it, but maybe it's just as well.

Arthur

40

From: Arthur Shilling [arthur.shilling@gammondhopes.com]
Sent: 12/21/2011 23.16 PM GMT
To: Steven Charteris [stevencharteris@staracademy.com]
Subject: The play's the thing

Steven

Today Jenny Barstiff (yes, she's still around which is more than I'll be shortly) told me that she'd heard Messrs Almoun, Rattles and Staffordshire discussing one Mr Shilling. I've been asked to attend a meeting this afternoon, so I could be in *Midsummer Night's Dream* without a job. Maybe I'll work at City Airport. I stare at the planes flying straight for our southern windows often enough. Maybe I could be a pilot or a steward.

First night tonight. My Bottom will not be a cheerful one.

Arthur Shilling

>

From: Steven Charteris [stevencharteris@staracademy.com]
Sent: 12/23/2011 10.16 AM GMT
To: Arthur Shilling [arthur.shilling@gammondhopes.com]
Subject: More of the best of times, the worst of times

Arthur

First things first. Seasons greetings and, yes, the Christmas tree arrived safely – although it wouldn't fit in our living room so it stands in the porch, decorated strangely (but interestingly) by Mrs C's fair hands.

Again I'm so apologetic that I won't be able make it to your play – circumstances dictated mostly through Mrs C's indisposition. We'd run out of her medication and, well, the risk was simply too great. I know that the play is on again in the New Year for a few days but, alas, I fear that we won't be able to venture south then either.

Well, a great deal to cover. Many of your recent experiences are really the buffeting of corporate life and you will have to get used to it. Some were not your fault and some, well – wrong place and wrong time. I have to say, from the evidence shown, that your writing is good and well done on what you have done well.

Press releases
- Press releases are fraught with difficulties, most easily solved. I know that you were writing releases and communications for internal use but the same broad principles apply.

- Headlines should be as short and interesting as possible and clearly contain the value of the press release to the reader.

- I get many press releases (yes, surprising isn't it, but that may be down to Mrs C's excesses) that are boring with paragraphs or even sentences containing lots of technical terms. These make me want to break things.

- I find that the biggest bugbear with press releases are the vague, nonsensical terms: leading, highly scaleable, holistic, end-to-end solution, innovative, a first – and other similar, pompous nonsense. Press releases should state what you want to say in as plain a language as you can.

- Bullet points at the top summarising the main points are helpful.

- Oh, yes. Try rewriting your first paragraph as a 'news in brief' item and put that in the email that introduces the press release.

- Once you've written your press release, go away and make a cup of tea. Come back and notice that the whole point of the release is in the last paragraph. This is because after writing seven paragraphs of waffle, you have a space of one-paragraph left in which to squeeze your essential information. Now make the last paragraph your introduction. It's a cliché, but the sting is often in the tail.

- Never write more than two pages – preferably keep it to just one. Two-hundred-and-fifty words is enough to say everything. Add a link to a longer email or source if there are specific details that need to be added.

- Only include a quote that someone might actually have said. Don't make one up to suit your story, particularly if he's your senior manager or Deputy Chairman! Don't quote people who aren't available for interview.

- Unnecessary graphics or big pictures just fill up my inbox, meaning that I might have to delete the release without reading it. If I want pictures I'll ask for them.

- Don't send out a release and then go on holiday for two weeks the next day. It's amazing how often this happens! It's very annoying if you need to speak to the author urgently.

Adding quotations to speeches

- Most people in an audience will forget 90 percent of a speech the morning after. But amazingly, people in the same audience can repeat a well-chosen quotation or humorous item from a speech, sometimes as long as several years later.

- If a quotation reinforces the point you want to make, it is almost impossible to misuse it. Used sparingly it is relatively easy to blend quotations into the natural flow of a speech. If the quotation is from someone the audience will respect, it gives credence to the main message.

- You don't have to use the whole quotation – as long as people understand the context and, again, relevance.

- Use quotations sparingly – they should support your speech and not the other way around.

- Always mention the author of the quotation. Only use a quotation if you are sure about the source *and* know how to pronounce the author's name. You could do more damage than good by misquoting a famous saying.

Report-writing

- Report-writing needs to be brief and to the point. The grammar should be perfect and the intent clear. The following quotes say it all really:

- "Reports can fulfill four different, and sometimes related, functions. They can be used as controls to ensure that all departments are functioning properly, to give information, to provide an analysis and to persuade others to act."

> — H. Dan O'Hair, James S. O'Rourke and Mary John O'Hair, *Business Communication: A Framework for Success*, South-Western College Publishing, 2001

- "For every long (formal) report, countless short (informal) reports lead to informed decisions on matters as diverse as the most comfortable office chairs to buy or the best recruit to hire for management training. Unlike long reports, most short reports require no extended planning, are quickly prepared, contain little or no background information and have no front or end matter (title page, table of contents, glossary and so on). But despite their conciseness, short reports do provide the information and analysis that readers need."

> — John M. Lannon, *Technical Communication*, Pearson, 2006

I think that I shall stop there. Again I'm very sorry that Mrs C and I couldn't see your undoubtedly great Bottom. With regards to your HR difficulties, sometimes blame does fall on our heads when it should not. Bullying and harassment are unacceptable and may, if they are allowed to go unchecked or are badly handled, create serious problems. I don't think this applies to you at all. You've made a few mistakes (dropping your boss in the doodoo by forgetting to edit his report wasn't exactly a positive note). But you will make more mistakes and your senior peers will (or should) recognise that we all make some. The key is to not make the same mistake twice.

A peck on the cheek from Mrs C and a pat on the back from me.

Kind regards

Professor S Charteris

Chapter Five

"Our remedies oft in ourselves do lie,
Which we ascribe to Heaven."

Helena: *All's Well That Ends Well* (I, i)

41

From: Arthur Shilling [arthur.shilling@gammondhopes.com]
Sent: 01/03/2012 05.16 AM GMT
To: Steven Charteris [stevencharteris@staracademy.com]
Subject: Some resolutions

Steven

Happy New Year. Thank you for your advice. Once again, all gratefully received. I'm glad that Mrs C is on the long road to recovery, but it must be really hard to have to hide everything with alcohol in it, including Marks & Spencer sherry trifle.

I do believe that all the recent hubub with regards to my misdemeanours has been put to one side. Jez is sort of acknowledging my existence and Mr Almoun doesn't exactly wink any more, but at least he engages me in dialogue and when he forgets himself, he shoots me with his fingers.

We've been told that our department has to go on a team-building exercise for two days somewhere in the depths of Wales. We have to be prepared for physical team-building. Jenny Barstiff says that she's not going and she's appealed to Mr Goodenhardt for support, but the lift conversation has it that their relationship has cooled and one suspects that the teary-eyed Jenny will shortly leave the world of GH. Mr Almoun has decreed that everyone *must* attend the offsite (for that's what it's called) and that no excuse will be sanctioned. You can almost see the whirrings of the mental machinations of people trying to construct an excuse that would be a) viable and b) more viable.

Mr Almoun called the department together – everyone was there, including seniors like Flattergleich, Rattles, Staffordshire and Bose. The presentation was short, but fervently delivered: "This is important everyone. Guys, this is crucial. Attendance is mandatory and success will go towards your end-of-year bonus consideration." He paused while everyone took that nugget in. All viable and non-viable excuses evaporated. "This exercise will be tough, agonising and, well, tough," he shouted. There was more in this vein along with joining and travel instructions, what to bring, what not, what attitudes and mindsets to have in place and so on *ad* fairly *infinitum*.

Mr F called me in for a briefing re a new event in which he's involved. He's asked me to attend in an advisory capacity. A new production agency was present, the main representative of which was dressed like a teenage clubber. He was in his early fifties and sporting a baggy white shirt and leather trousers which creaked if he as much as tickled his nose. At one point in the meeting, his trousers let out such a squeal that we all looked on in great alarm. Around his neck he wore leather thongs with peace symbol jewellery. When called upon to say anything – credentials, view on the succinct brief produced by Mr F and yours truly or to advise on content and structure, Mr Lammon would clear his throat as if he was about to eject some terrible mucus from his throat. After an hour Mr F could take it no longer: "*Genug ist genug danken Ihnen.*" ("Enough is enough thank you.") He glared at Mr Lammon, but the man took little notice and continued in leather-creaking and expectorating fashion.

New auditions next week just before our offsite trip to Wales. We're putting on *Coriolanus*, a bit bloody in my view and also with few laughs, but everyone's very keen. I wonder, should I go for the big one now?

Yours in Roman mood,

Arthur

42

From: Arthur Shilling [arthur.shilling@gammondhopes.com]
Sent: 01/10/2012 20.16 PM GMT
To: Steven Charteris [stevencharteris@staracademy.com]
Subject: Off we go

Steven

Tomorrow we're off to Wales. Going in a coach which will undoubtedly make me queasy (remember that trip to Stratford?). We still have no real information about our tasks although I do know that I'm sharing a small room with Jenny (!) and Jez Staffordshire (yikes!). That'll make for interesting night times.

Mrs Sourdough has tried every trick in the book to excuse herself, but Mr Almoun is having none of it. In a mock Scottish accent he pranced around her desk, shouting, "If ye dinna turrrn up, why then Missie, tha shall have nae good marrrks on your end o' year review, will ye noo?" Mrs Sourdough tried to say "I don't think, Mr Almoun, you can say things like that", by which time our prancing leader had danced off down the line of desks whistling *Scotland the Brave*. Who knows why? Maybe he thinks Wales is in the north rather than westerly. Good job the Normans didn't make that same mistake.

Yours aye

McArthur

43

From: Arthur Shilling [arthur.shilling@gammondhopes.com]
Sent: 01/13/2012 18.16 PM GMT
To: Steven Charteris [stevencharteris@staracademy.com]
Subject: Teamwork works – on occasion

Steven

Well now. The Welsh experiment failed miserably although Mr Almoun thinks that it was a rip-roaring success.

We arrived in the middle of the Welsh mountains at around 10PM, tired and not a little fed up. Mr Almoun had tried (certainly until Bristol) to instill some camaraderie into the proceedings with intercontinental scouting songs – no real enthusiasm amongst the 'team' for that. Our transport, by the way, was one of those huge coaches in which highly paid footballers travel. The windows were dark so nobody could see in and the seating arrangement was that of a private jet. There was a washroom on board along with a kitchen and a hostess who smelled strongly of alcohol. We were served a picnic lunch although most of the team had such picky eating habits which Jenny Barstiff had failed to ascertain properly beforehand (as had been asked of her) that there was a pile of uneaten sandwiches. She had also managed to get the soft drinks order wrong – as a result most of us had small boxes of coconut milk upon which to sup.

On arrival at the Team Winning Camp, Welsh Division, we were quickly escorted to our huts (aka dormitories) and told to get some sleep by a very large lady wearing a bright red jumpsuit. My small group – consisting, as mentioned, of Jenny, Jez and self – shuffled around the tiny hut looking for places to put our meagre luggage, although Jenny's was anything but meagre. The beds were of the flimsy camping variety and Jenny and I immediately feared for Jez's safety. "I can't sleep on dat," said the dismayed Jez. However, understanding quickly that there was no alternative and realising that our wake-up call was to be at 4AM, we managed to settle down with the minimum of nudity and, as far as Jez was concerned, thank the heavens was all I could whisper. Jenny was another matter altogether of course and her shapely form shall remain locked on my retinas for some time hence.

The next day passed in a whirl of crises. Our first task (before any breakfast I might point out) was to jog around the camp shouting out ludicrous American army slogans, accompanied by an ex US marine called DeWight. DeWight took an instant shine to Jenny and the opposite to poor Jez. After the 'run' we were told to grab a hunk of bread and a mug of sweet tea and sit in our groups to plan how to use six planks and a rubber ring plus assortments of rope to get the three of us across a babbling brook (which was actually not babbling so much as roaring and at least five metres wide at its narrowest point). Having discussed all options, we began to build our raft, Jenny and I making regular eye contact indicating that we had no clue a) what we were doing or b) how we could possibly transport the large and puffing Jez in or on our flimsy craft.

When our seamanship was put to the test, I got Jenny safely across and went back for a nervous Jez. "Oh my," he said repeatedly. The camp was watching and waiting for here was a spectacle to behold and fun to boot. All the camp employees came along to look (jeer and leer) as well. It was abundantly clear that our small craft just wasn't going to work so I asked Jez to gently lie flat on his back on the middle planks while I held the raft firm. I then immersed myself in the freezing early January Welsh water and swam the craft across. Apart from a few lurches and exhortations from Jez to "take care, please take care, I can't swim, I can't truly", we managed to get to the other side, although I swallowed far more of the sheep-dipped water than was probably good for one. Once the raft hit the other bank, Jez began to sit up and, such was his anxiety to maintain terra firma, that he scrambled up and off, using my head as a stepping stone. How everyone laughed. Jez was a hero and I, well, I was a bedraggled and gasping mess. Only the massive DeWight helped me out of the water. He looked me in the eye and said, "Good job there son, good job", or 'some such thing' and turned away to shout at Mr Flattergleich who was cross because his brand new boots were dirty.

That morning brought more delights. There was archery and then a paintball war during which Mrs Sourdough burst into tears mainly, it was thought, because of the mud. After a lunch of baked beans on toast, a bag of strange flavoured crisps and some warm orange juice in a small box but no straw, we were taken to the meditation room where we were taught how to meditate, except that six of us went to sleep. Jez moaned in his snoozing state and one can only imagine that rafting demons were revisiting him once again.

I won't regale you with everything because I sense that you'd be mightily bored. Suffice it to say, nobody really had a wonderful time, although Mr Almoun was in his element, dancing about with perpetual glee on his face.

For now, kind regards

Arthur

44

From: Arthur Shilling [arthur.shilling@gammondhopes.com]
Sent: 01/22/2012 19.16 PM GMT
To: Steven Charteris [stevencharteris@staracademy.com]
Subject: A verbal duel

Steven

I received a card from Jez saying thanks for saving his life. I do believe that any misdemeanours in the past have been expunged by that raft incident. My cup, for a moment, ran over only to be thrown rather heavily to the floor via the ire of Mr F who has to present to the Chairman's committee on the year's work in global group communications. Apparently, I'd received an email instructing me to work with Mr F on a PowerPoint presentation days before

Wales and indeed I had – but had totally forgotten to attend the meeting and had equally therefore done nothing to assist.

Mr Bose says that you can't win them all although, in his view, winning Jez's devotion must count for a great deal. I have to see Mr F tomorrow. Apparently (fortuitously) the Chairman's committee meeting has been put back so I have some time to repair the damage.

Coriolanus has been abandoned (being too full of blood and guts as well as being a touch too serious) and we are to do the Scottish play instead – as if that's a bundle of laughs! I have always thought *Macbeth* one of Shakespeare's darkest plays so I'm not a hundred percent sure of the thinking here. Still, there's more for me to chew on here – parts-wise that is – and I'm quite keen to have a bash at Banquo, although I would miss any activity in the second half of the play unless I was to play a spear-holding warrior or something. Graham Graveling (my friend and fellow thespian who was an excellent rude mechanical in *Midsummer Night's Dream*) says that I could consider the title role but, when I told Jenny Barstiff, she rather unkindly laughed like a drain and said that I'd be better suited as a witch. Jenny studied *Macbeth* at school and annoyingly knew much of the text by heart, so we began a duel: "Fair is foul, and foul is fair", and I replied in similar vein. This went on for half an hour until there came there a shout of irritation from Mrs Sourdough, "Oh for goodness' sake!" she said crossly, "Some of us have duties to perform!" There was a hush and then Jenny muttered (under her breath), "Something wicked this way comes." And we giggled and went our ways.

Best

Arthur

45

From: Arthur Shilling [arthur.shilling@gammondhopes.com]
Sent: 01/28/2012 19.16 PM GMT
To: Steven Charteris [stevencharteris@staracademy.com]
Subject: PowerPoint rears its head

Steven

My meeting with Mr Flattergleich was sombre. He has changed certainly – his accent is much improved in the sense that he speaks more clearly and his English pronunciation is more appropriate for British and international financial audiences. He has apparently had some presentation coaching which has paid dividends. PowerPoint, however, is still not his strong suit. Is it anyone's?

I received the initial "I was most disappointed…" and "Sometimes you trust a person and sometimes that person lets you down…" and, "I vunder, Shilling, if you are up to this…" Anyway, once all this was out of the way, we sat down with a PowerPoint designer (and thank any deity you care to mention because I am not a whiz when it comes to wretched PowerPoint).

However, the meeting continued badly with Mr F insisting that pages and pages of Franklin Gothic Medium font size 12 text should be included in his Chairman's committee presentation. Four hours later (honestly!) we had persuaded Mr F that big font bullet points would work. We also agreed that, if the Chairman's PA had said that there was a half-hour slot, then a two-and-a-half-hour presentation would not do. Mr F said that he would rely on our good endeavours to reduce the hours to thirty minutes and that we should meet in a few days to rehearse. We stood and stretched. I said apropos nothing, "Screw your courage to the sticking-place." There was a pause and some boggle-eyed staring. "Lady Macbeth, Act I, scene vii,' I said somewhat lamely as I left the room.

Arthur

P.S. I swear as I left Mr F's office I heard an accented rendition of "Life's but a walking shadow, a poor player / That struts and frets his hour upon the stage, / And then is heard no more. It is a tale / Told by an idiot, full of sound and fury, / Signifying nothing." I walked on and off to lunch. I could have also sworn that I heard him sigh heavily at the quote's end.

46

From: Arthur Shilling [arthur.shilling@gammondhopes.com]
Sent: 02/06/2012 23.16 PM GMT
To: Steven Charteris [stevencharteris@staracademy.com]
Subject: PowerPoint rears its head again

Steven

We had a good run through of Mr F's presentation. The Chairman has sent word that he wants to discuss another 'where will the world be in thirty years' type of event. It's to be mooted at the committee meeting at which Mr F is presenting. So, panic from the German quarter – much Goethe quoted, some Wagner sung and a huge telling off for anyone who had the temerity that day to interrupt our proceedings. The visage was dreadful to behold and Mr F's normally tidy office was a desolated beach of a room with smoking holes from various explosions. Well, the rehearsal worked (in the end) moderately well with the PowerPoint designer guy threatening resignation only twice. Moods were placated and coffee drunk. Chocolate biscuits were shared. And then Mr Goodenhardt knocked and came in all smiles and false beams. "All well I trust dear Hermann?" said he. "Big day next Tuesday. It'll be perfect," and then Mr G swept us mere mortals with a malign smile. Mr F looked a little deflated after the interruption.

I've got Banquo! Actually I'm quite pleased and really in my heart of hearts I knew that I couldn't have played the title role – as indeed our lisping friend who got the part can't. I suspect foul deeds. I can make Banquo strong and meaningful. Didn't you play Banquo once back in the day? Or was that Mrs C?

Oh, by the way, Chloe from Corporate PR came to say hello this morning and actually pecked me on the cheek when she left. On reflection she came to see me for no real reason other than to ascertain if I was comfortable with giving a speech on the retirement of Mr Terry Nugget, someone whom I don't know but whose retirement is imminent. Apparently, it's a tradition for a newbie to say fare thee well to an oldie. I didn't even think about what I'd agreed to until the fragrant Chloe had wafted off.

Arthur

47

From: Arthur Shilling [arthur.shilling@gammondhopes.com]
Sent: 02/19/2012 23.16 PM GMT
To: Steven Charteris [stevencharteris@staracademy.com]
Subject: PowerPoint my oh my

Steven

So Mr F did his thing in front of the Chairman and what happened is only related by Mr Bose and a little by Mr Rattles who were both present. Apparently, Mr F began well. His accent remained contained and his pace was reasonably brisk. His points were strong and the PowerPoint – now redolent in its simplicity – moved along in sharp precision. (The PowerPoint guy had done a good job.) After five minutes all was well until the Chairman interrupted and asked a question. Then all hell broke loose.

Mr F was surprised at the question (which was apparently reasonably innocuous – something about projected budgets). He stopped in mid-flow and looked surprised and not a little hurt. He answered the question and the Chairman seemed comfortable with the answer, indicating with a brusque 'thank you' that our hero should continue. However, Mr F was lost. He clicked his clicker three or four times, moving his content to a point that was way ahead of where he thought he was or wanted to be. There then was a mad scramble by Mr F as he tried to reverse the situation by pressing another button. That not working, he let out a few *'got in himmels'* and *'ve get zis in ein moment'*. But the moment was lost and the presentation descended into apologies and half-heard truths about the position of the company's global communications. Luckily, and this was a saving grace, we had prepared a handout which (I like to think) set out exactly that which the PowerPoint had failed to deliver. Mr Bose's comment on the handout was that it was "perfect and most welcome".

The Chairman apparently showed little in the way of any anger or frustration and Mr Rattles believes that he must get used to appalling presentations. The Chairman's main interest was a discussion of his 'what's the world going to be like in x years' time?' event – a replication of the Executive Forum in which I was involved. Apparently, Mr F salvaged much of the situation by discussing the Chairman's project with ease and sense. The Chairman was seen to nod appreciatively and Mr F was not sent to some deep GH dungeon with only bread and water, much to the chagrin of Mr Goodenhardt who, on hearing of the presentation's 'demise', was almost breaking open the champagne to celebrate his own promotion. Mr Bose, in relating this bit of info, looked cross.

When I next met Mr F a day later, he was not angry, but relieved. He asked me to arrange PowerPoint instruction for the whole department and insisted that everybody (including Mrs Sourdough) should understand how to use our laptops for presentation purposes.

Rehearsals have begun with the Scottish play. I've decided to make Banquo distinguished and reliable on the one hand but, on the other, hurt and distressed. I want the audience to believe that there are secret and hidden depths to Banquo's character. Our director, Linda Nookles, wants to put the thing in modern dress which is odd and something I always find inexplicable. Jenny is in the play as well and is playing Lady Macduff. She's magnificent. Our lisping friend has fallen head over heels with Jenny B but she dismisses him with a mere flick of an imperial hand.

Best to you and kind regards to Mrs C, whom I hope is much recovered.

Arthur the Wraith

48

From: Arthur Shilling [arthur.shilling@gammondhopes.com]
Sent: 02/26/2012 22.16 PM GMT
To: Steven Charteris [stevencharteris@staracademy.com]
Subject: Retirement speeches aren't so bad

Steven

Yesterday evening I gave my speech in honour of the old codger who was retiring after 33 years with the bank. 'Old codger' is a bit mean because he is a nice enough soul. He said, privately, that he'd wanted to retire for years and had hoped to have been made redundant with attendant pay out, but there you are, you can't have it all and, anyway, life had been kind. His wife was in attendance, all pearls and lipstick and the canapés were decent enough, although Jez Staffordshire wore one on his shirt front for most of the evening.

My speech was regarded as short and erudite (mercifully, since Mr Rattles had already spent twenty yawning minutes detailing every single one of the gent's achievements). I used no notes, having rehearsed and really 'learnt my part'. I only included one innocuous joke about a wasp and a pot of jam which was reasonably witty and caused the company to chuckle in a good humoured 'thank goodness the joke's done but please don't let Mr Shilling tell another' sort of way. Mr Bose muttered a 'well done' afterwards and Mrs Sourdough asked me to dance even though there was no music or dancing opportunity. Our Deputy Chairman, Sir Christopher, thanked the speakers although he called me 'Spilling' and he added a few words as well, most sentences beginning with 'aaaahm'. But, by and large, a pleasant evening all round.

I have been told that there's a new newbie joining the department and I'm to look after him since I'm no longer regarded as a newbie. His name's Gordon Lock and, for some reason, the name rings a bell.

I have also been told by Dephne Hong that we are to gather arms and begin plans for a new 'where will the world be in many years hence' series of events for middle management across the globe. Our kickoff meeting is next week. Sounds good. Dubai's on the cards as is Hong Kong next and then I think London again.

Best

Arthur

49

From: Arthur Shilling [arthur.shilling@gammondhopes.com]
Sent: 03/06/2012 19.16 AM GMT
To: Steven Charteris [stevencharteris@staracademy.com]
Subject: Shakespeare

Steven

The new newbie has arrived and, of course, I remember exactly who he is. He's that chap you chucked out of your seminars for cheek or similar offences. Reckoned he knew more about Shakespeare than you and half the academics in most of the world's universities.

"Ah, Shilling, for I thought 'twas you," said Gordon Lock. "I'm yours for the duration I understand and you can teach me all you know which," here he smiled sidelong at Mrs Sourdough (who I'm grateful to report was unimpressed), "I suspect isn't a right lot." He then spent much of the day telling me and anyone else in proximity how Shakespeare infuses our daily lives, whether we care to see it or not. He went on to tell anyone that the Bard perfected narrative conventions seen everywhere in film and in literature, pronounced by Gordon as *Lit. Er. Rat. Your.*

Gordon is one of these people who are absurdly confident, but to the point of arrogance and people either warm to this or loathe it – there's no middle ground. Mr Bose loathed it and Jez warmed. I loathed and Jenny B warmed. Whenever I tried to help make Gordon's induction as pleasant as possible, I failed since he took no real notice and paid scant attention. Even Mrs Sourdough snapped at a very early level and muttered, "that boy, waste of time or some such thing" on several occasions.

Gordon, for some reason (possibly because he had spent two weeks in Greece during the summer at his parents' villa) consistently played Greek music on his iPod but with the volume so high that the whole room could more or less hear the yowl caused by an imagined cat with its tail caught in the spokes of a bicycle. The 'music' may have gone down well in Sparta or Thessalonki but it wasn't a hit in Canary Wharf. The fabulous Mr Bose had a word in Gordon's ear and the young fellow looked genuinely alarmed but whatever was said had the right effect. We heard no more Greek wailing.

The first meeting for the Chairman's 'what's the world likely to be like etc.' event took place with Deaf Knee in the lead and me sitting at her left side. Gordon Lock was shadowing me so he was glued to my right filling in doodles of strange animals that he'd drawn on his pad. He'd also written 'GL is a rock god'. We had the communications agency and their creatives in tow – all leather satchels and designer jeans with lots of spectacles being taken on and off and the flicking of lank hair all over the place. Deaf Knee was superb, having had a close briefing from the Chairman and Mr Flattergleich. She was concise, precise and even less hesitant in her speech pattern. Gordon began finishing her sentences for her which received smiles from the agency until Deaf Knee gently put down her pencil, smacked the table hard with both hands and said to Gordon quietly and with no small menace, "What is your problem?" That received a smirk from Gordon and a sharp intake of breath from the agency notables who, I'm pleased to say, looked a little taken back. Gordon whispered "weirdo" into my ear and whether Dephne heard that or not, the meeting continued uninterrupted. Dubai is indeed first port of call and we're to try and get hold of as many speakers who contributed to the original Forum as possible. That's my role. Production values are to be higher with lighting moods and themed environments – and this time there will an allocation for breakout sessions and deeper engagement in some of the core topics.

Mr Goodenhardt came up to me yesterday afternoon to enquire as to how Mr F was 'getting on'. I had no idea what to say and so replied, "Very well, Mr Goodenhardt, very well thank you." Mr G looked at me oddly and then said, "I understand that you thespians are giving us *Macbeth*? Well, one can learn from that most certainly." With that he darted into a lift and was gone. Out of the lift came Sir Christopher, our Deputy Chairman, and he actually said, "Good afternoon, Henry," which made me feel a) one of the in-crowd and b) one of the outsiders since he clearly thought I was someone else.

Best,

Arthur (Henry) Shilling

50

From: Arthur Shilling [arthur.shilling@gammondhopes.com]
Sent: 03/09/2012 19.16 PM GMT
To: Steven Charteris [stevencharteris@staracademy.com]
Subject: Cold

Dear Steven

I cannot write much or indeed anything as am bed with severe chill and am being nursed by Nurse Holyhead, although she has already dropped green medicine on my pyjamas. Florence Nightingale she is not.

I have the ague and maybe the plague too for all I know.

More anon.

Arthur

>

From: Steven Charteris [stevencharteris@staracademy.com]
Sent: 03/15/2012 07.16 AM GMT
To: Arthur Shilling [arthur.shilling@gammondhopes.com]
Subject: Cold comfort farm

Dear Arthur

Firstly, Mrs C was very grateful for your concern about her health. She is getting better thank you and her intake of her medications (various) is somewhat diminished. Secondly, we both hope that *you* are now fully recovered from your chill and we must all take solace from the fact that you were in good and safe hands.

You've had a very busy time and I'm delighted that you're regarded as part of the team. You've clearly matured in your outlook and, by the sound of it, your senior colleagues recognise the same.

I was really heartened to learn of your courage in Wales. What you did was very beneficial to your career and showed a good side of your character. I believe, from what you said, that Mr Staffordshire was very grateful and he won't forget that in a hurry. I also suspect that he will have told others of your 'deed'.

I'm sure that the position with Mr Flattergleich will improve. Don't forget that you've worked together fairly closely on presentations and scripts and it's quite normal for someone in his position to vent his spleen on someone in yours. I suspect that he likes you and respects what you do to support him. Importantly, he now needs to fully understand PowerPoint and, of course, how to control the machinery that presents it.

Let's spend a bit of time on PowerPoint, since it's a perennial problem and a pain in the behind for most people in business and there are some who simply ignore the most basic of rules:

PowerPoint

- A PowerPoint presentation isn't a 'must' whenever a presentation is made. You can speak without one like all politicians do, as do presidents and many business people. If PowerPoint is used it is there only to *support* what is being said. Nothing more.

- Less is more in a slide show. Too much information on a single slide becomes unreadable. Content should be presented in the form of four to five bulleted points per slide; anything more and you end up creating clutter. Using bullets not only makes a slide readable, but it also adds to the overall impact of a presentation.

- Make bullets visible and use short sentences or phrases. Limit each to six words in one line and space the text/bullet points out evenly.

- Contrast the text with the background, but be wary of using every colour in the spectrum.

- To highlight certain important information, present that text in a larger font size.

- Keep to the same font. Don't start to jazz up the presentation or make it too animated.

- While I dislike PowerPoint intensely, it does offer multimedia capabilities – but don't get carried away with flashy videos, music clips or graphics. One of my students made a presentation on Dickens' London. It was a serious topic, but every slide had background music and every other click of the mouse produced fancy effects. This detracted from the subject being discussed. I also think that he was infatuated with Little Dorrit.

So, use the multimedia capabilities only for special emphasis or to demonstrate how something works. Excessive animation is puerile and of little use. Leave that to designers who can't really design, much like marketers who can't really market. They always hide behind excessive graphics as much as they do nonsensical phrases and empty promises.

Presenting with PowerPoint

- Your PowerPoint presentation should not be confused with a teleprompter, i.e. any presenter should never read aloud word for word what's on the screen. It's so lazy – not to mention insulting to the audience. People will yawn and yearn for coffee and a chance to rush to the car park and go home.

- Make sure that you're not blocking the audience's view. Use a laser beam to identify the points on the screen if you really must, but never your arm. A flailing arm is a distraction and looks moderately stupid. I do have a colleague (you will know him Arthur) who insists that his students read the PowerPoint, but he refuses to move away from the screen. As a consequence, the students read the slides from his face.

- Go slowly but not too slowly. There's nothing worse than a speaker droning on and on when the audience has long got the point. Similarly, it's a total waste of time if a presenter goes too quickly, losing the audience and its interest along the way. Much of this is down to understanding who your audience is and what its members know.

- Rehearse and rehearse some more. Executives seem to think that they can look at their PowerPoint two minutes before showtime and deliver a credible presentation. Well, I've never heard of anyone ever who can do that.

- If you are uncertain about a PowerPoint presentation, perhaps you could run it past a colleague or a friend. Mr Bose I imagine would give you time and I suspect the lovely Mrs Sourdough would as well. Ask them for feedback. Recollect all the presentations you attended – what you liked about them, what you disliked about them and so on – although I would rather that you kept any adverse comments about mine to yourself if you please.

- PowerPoint may be a great piece of technology, but the effectiveness of your 'client' as a public speaker will eventually dictate the impact. Not the wretched PowerPoint!

Macbeth is a great play of course, but a hard one to deliver well, so I wish you good fortune. Banquo's a good part and I know that you won't 'overdo it'. Subtelty has its charm.

Mrs C is doing better on a daily basis and we must hope that she doesn't dive back down into the depths. I won't, if you don't mind, offer to bring her along to see your play. I suspect that madness will be that much sooner upon her if I do and I fret about the effect Lady McB or indeed the witches will have on her sensitive soul.

Kind regards as always and keep up the good work. Oh, yes, before I forget – I do remember that wretched Gordon whatsit. Nasty piece of work as I recall, with a very poor third to his 'credit' and that only by the grace of Professor Marshall who knew his father. I can't imagine where he'll end up, but his papa is loaded and so I don't really care overmuch.

Regards

Professor Charteris

Chapter Six

"A horse, a horse, my kingdom for a horse."

Richard III: *Richard III* (V, iv)

51

From: Arthur Shilling [arthur.shilling@gammondhopes.com]
Sent: 03/24/2012 05.16 AM GMT
To: Steven Charteris [stevencharteris@staracademy.com]
Subject: Drinks party

Steven

Again, thank you so very much for your wise words. Much appreciated. Please thank Mrs C for the kind gift of thick climbing socks. Despite the size, they will come in very handy if and when I try to attack Everest (or indeed revisit Wales). It was a very thoughtful gesture, one for which I most grateful. Please also tell her that I am much recovered to rude health and would only wish her the same.

Yesterday evening I attended a departmental drinks party to which partners (wives, girlfriends, husbands, boyfriends and similar) were invited. I brought along my landlady, Victoria Holyhead, because she was at a loose end and she's also good fun and gregarious. When we arrived, the guests were both surprised and heartened at my choice of partner and, within moments, all and sundry were tripping over themselves to supply my redheaded friend with drinks and small, tasty morsels.

"She's OK, Arthur," said oily Gordon, who'd brought along a very dreary looking girl in some sort of kaftan outfit and whose name was unpronounceable. "Out of your league, Gordon and don't embarrass me," I retorted. "My league, dear boy, is premiership. Manchester United is my league as is the part of Macbeth. Say hello to your new lead." "What?" squeaked I. "Yes," he went on in his oily way. "Your lisping friend had to withdraw and, well, I suggested my good self for the part, did an audition for your Linda Nookles and, well, there you are. The part is mine. You're comfortable with that I'm sure. Now I really feel that I should say hello to your delightful landlady. Bye." Steven, my heart grew cold with a) hate, b) more hate and c) misery.

Mr Goodenhardt was at the party with his wife. She is a tall, gaunt woman with thin lips and was sporting a turquoise dress with a strange flower pattern. Mr G made a beeline for Mr Rattles and they stood in a corner talking urgently like a couple of Roman conspirators. I went over to Mrs G to make idle conversation. She wasn't exactly welcoming, but I snatched a glass of Prosecco Treviso from a passing waiter and offered it to the lady. She accepted the glass gracefully enough. She had a tiny speck of cream cheese on a corner of her thin mouth and I did debate whether to tell her but fear won. "I worry about my husband you know," she said after the pleasantries had been made. "He was a rising star back in New York, but suddenly lost his way for some reason. We don't have children you know." I tried to absorb both facts simultaneously and was filled with wild surmise. I said nothing but nodded. "I prod him on you know," she said. "He really should be Global Head of Communications of course.

Everyone thinks so, but that German sticks to the job with grim perseverance. What do *you* think of Mr Flattergleich?" Before I could answer, she went on, "I am urging my husband to definitive action. We will win this battle. We will achieve success and then it will be back to New York." She stared at me and I stared at the facial cream cheese. She spoke in a softer voice, "I understand that you're in that Scottish play. I saw a production in New York. Very interesting how Lady Macbeth managed to persuade her husband to action. Ultimate action." Her eyes went misty, her lips became thinner still, her nostrils dilated. I was at a loss but was saved by the re-emergence of Mr G who ignored me totally and steered his wife in the direction of someone else.

Jenny Barstiff seemed rather the worse for wear. "That dreadful Gordon thing," she burbled, "is going to ruin the play. You do realise? He's got to go." I replied, "I thought you liked him." "No," she said quite brusquely, "My heart is set on another." She twirled, smiled and jetted off. I collected a rather tipsy landlady and we made our way home.

Regards

Arthur

52

From: Arthur Shilling [arthur.shilling@gammondhopes.com]
Sent: 04/02/2012 10.16 AM GMT
To: Steven Charteris [stevencharteris@staracademy.com]
Subject: Dubai

Steven

I have prepared most of the agenda for the first of the new 'How the world's going to be in 2030' Forum for our Chairman. The event is to be termed the Chairman's Strategic Forum now – more sensible thinks Mr Bose.

I'm off to Dubai in a few days and we're going to stay in a smart five-star hotel in the Jumeirah Beach area. Deaf Knee's going tomorrow with a couple of colleagues and the production mob. I had a script meeting with the Chairman's PA to discuss his (new and updated) opening address. Unfortunately, I had to take the wretched Gordon with me who had no interest in anything going on. He is basking in his lead role in the play and rehearsals are ghastly affairs with him giving a view on any aspect of anyone's character. I suspect that even our esteemed director is beginning to fray around the edges.

Bumped into Jackie Gershwin, she with the vast nose. She's doing some Strategic Forum research for Dephne Hong. I can't listen to JG without regarding the nose.

We had a meeting with the Chairman's PA, who's a smart chap with pure intelligence writ large over his face. He listened to my comments about the speech, nodded, made some notes, commented here and there and then said, "Well I'm comfortable with this Arthur. Do you have everything you need?" At which point Gordon, who'd been moodily picking his nails and nose, yawned hugely without putting his hand in front of his mouth. The PA looked up sharply and said nothing but rose quickly, shook hands with me and was gone. "That was very rude," said I to Gordon. "Yeah," he drawled, "So? This is all so deadly dull and sooo boring."

He's not one of us you know.

Regards

Arthur

53

From: Arthur Shilling [arthur.shilling@gammondhopes.com]
Sent: 04/06/2012 08.16 AM GMT
To: Steven Charteris [stevencharteris@staracademy.com]
Subject: The Middle East

Steven

Well Dubai is a) hot and b) exciting. Settled in at the hotel and all the rooms, including the auditorium, are brilliant. We'll have three separate shows with 400 people at each. The set's gone up and everything's looking great. The air conditioning is brilliant and the food extraordinarily good. We were given a very warm welcome by our Regional General Manager, who spent the whole of my first evening briefing me on a) Dubai and b) his family. Two hours later I came to the conclusion that a) was interesting and b) was not.

Deaf Knee has everything under tight control. The first event is to be in the company of one of the Royal Princes and we are obliged to have a row of forty thrones with very high backs right in front of the front row of chairs. This is so that the Prince and his entourage can be seated with an obvious bird's eye view. However, it does mean of course that the second row through to the thirtieth won't be able to see anything – certainly up until coffee time when it was mooted that the Prince and entourage might think of leaving. The event's producer was throwing his weight all over the place and snapping his fingers at his team and crew. He snapped his fingers at me and I decided to 'do' a Dephne Hong. I stared at him with cold contempt and he actually apologised! There's only one person who gets away with snapping his fingers at me and that's Mr Almoun and the Chairman I suppose if he so chose to snap an odd finger in my direction.

Our guest speakers are all in, fed and watered. The Chairman's arriving in a while and I'm expected to be part of the welcoming committee, so I'd better go.

Regards to both you and your Sultana.

Arthur

54

From: Arthur Shilling [arthur.shilling@gammondhopes.com]
Sent: 04/07/2012 09.16 AM GMT
To: Steven Charteris [stevencharteris@staracademy.com]
Subject: Sharia law

Steven

The difficult thing here is that we have to incorporate local specialists into the speaker mix and that's proven to be something of a tough task. For instance, I've been told that we need a speaker on Sharia law. Sharia law is the code of law derived from the Koran and from the teachings and example of Mohammed. Sharia prohibits the payment or acceptance of specific interest or fees (known as *Riba* or *usury*) for loans of money. Investing in businesses that provide goods or services considered contrary to Islamic principles is forbidden. There are also rules as to how women might and might not interface with finance. It's rather complex but the local managers have been very helpful and I have some good leads.

Jenny emailed to say that the *Macbeth* production was lurching from crisis to crisis with Gordon oblivious to anyone else but him and his role. Gorgeous Lady Macbeth has apparently twice threatened to resign her part. Jenny has dropped hints to anyone who cares to listen that Gordon isn't perhaps cut out for international finance or indeed the Scottish throne.

I've been told by Mr Derek Rattles that so impressed was he by my landlady, Victoria Holyhead (whom Mr R apparently refers to as 'our Vicky'), he's asked her to develop a makeup exercise for the department, details to be issued forthwith. I won't invite her back to a company 'do' in a hurry. Apparently we have to be made up so that facially we take on the characteristics of an animal and have to relate to one another as those animals for a day. Mr Almoun will decide with Mr R who will be what animal. So that's something wonderful to which we must look forward then!

Miaow or, better, grrrr

Arthur

55

From: Arthur Shilling [arthur.shilling@gammondhopes.com]
Sent: 04/10/2012 08.16 AM GMT
To: Steven Charteris [stevencharteris@staracademy.com]
Subject: Back home

Steven

I'm led to believe that Dubai was a success, which is a relief. However, I came back to a Gordon whose popularity has sunk to such a low that nobody really wants to help him or his induction. I also understand that *Macbeth* is on the verge of collapse – not a good thing since our small theatre group, The Shakedown Players, gets funded by the company and a failed play would not look good for future investment. Our director, Linda Nookles, is in bits.

Mr Almoun has told us all what our makeup animals are to be. I'm a tiger, which is rather good and Gordon is a mongoose, which is a hoot. What my landlady ('our Vicky') will do is to make masks which she will then glue onto our faces with a special experimental silicone glue which only she can remove – a factor insisted upon by Mr Almoun who wants nobody to chicken out (haha). She has been in to measure our faces, causing much raucous laughter from Gordon and Mrs Sourdough – for very different reasons. Apparently Mr Rattles has agreed a fee for Ms Holyhead of voluminous proportions. I'm hoping that I might get a long rent-free period as a result of my introduction. Mrs Sourdough is a little put out that she's to be a chicken and Jez Staffordshire is very, very put out to learn that he's to be a wild boar. 'Ahem' is all I can say.

My landlady dislikes Gordon even more than she did when he grabbed her arm and attention at our drinks party. When she was measuring his face, he apparently made all sorts of unreasonable and unsavoury suggestions. Came the day for our fitting and the department was full of excited chatter. At around 10AM, everyone's faces (bar Mr Bose's because he was – luckily – on leave) were festooned with appropriate masks and many a giggle and occasional shriek was to be had. We were meant to interact with one another as would our 'characters'. My role allowed me to growl nastily at most people and pretend that I was about to devour them whole. Unfortunately, Mr Almoun had not told any other department in the building what we were up to and there were emails and phone calls galore to Mr Flattergleich complaining about the 'nonsense in the comms department'. Mr Alan Trebbish, our senior receptionist, was most put out when an elephant and a gorilla whistled past him at lunchtime.

The day wore on midst much hilarity until the appointed time to have the masks removed and indeed all were removed – except Gordon's. My landlady seemed to have forgotten him and had left before the twit realised. There ensued much shouting from about how he would get my landlady and rip her head off. Mr Almoun had a warning word about parliamentary language and, although Gordon had quietened down, he was still in a state. So funny!

Just before home time, I was asked to join Deaf Knee at an impromptu Chairman's committee meeting to discuss the next Strategic Forum in Hong Kong. And Gordon was to come along too. Well, he wept, yelped and squealed and wept some more, but he had no real choice. As we joined the Chairman in his suite, Gordon was hovering behind my back but Mr Flattergleich insisted that he be introduced to our Chairman. There was a sudden silence as our leader took in the young man with a mongoose's head mask standing before him. "I see," said the Chairman, not really seeing at all, but having experienced most odd customs of the world in his lifetime. "And you come from where exactly, Mr ah, Mongoose?" I had to bite hard on my lower lip. There came a muffled something from behind Gordon's mask and then he fled the room and, I'm delighted to say, the company.

Suffice it say our lisping friend was cajoled back into the role of Macbeth and all was calm once more, although I have been asked to be less of a passionate ghost and a little more subtle.

Regards to Mrs C who I understand has taken a dip for the worse. More of the same?

Best

Arthur

56

From: Arthur Shilling [arthur.shilling@gammondhopes.com]
Sent: 04/15/2012 19.16 PM GMT
To: Steven Charteris [stevencharteris@staracademy.com]
Subject: Hard work

Steven

Not only do I have to prepare for Hong Kong, Mr F wants me to write two speeches in quick time. I also had to meet a delegation from a Chinese bank this morning and that wasn't as plain sailing as it sounds.

The bank gets visitors all of the time – business and political dignitaries and, occasionally, heads of state. On each occasion, the visitors are welcomed by at least three or four members of bank staff who escort them in a special lift to the 41st floor where there is a huge meeting room for special meetings. Just outside the room there is a large room where coffee, tea or drinks are served, depending on the time of day. It is in this room that the Chairman, Deputy Chairman or one of the divisional CEOs meets said important folk. Sometimes, if the visitors are very, very important then the Chairman will be at the front door standing close to Mr Alan Trebbish in case there's a need for receptionist advice.

Anyway, my visitors were from a bank, but still important nonetheless. I had been well tutored in how to present my business card and to whom and in what order of seniority. I knew the 'form' so I was reasonably confident about the task and thought little of it. The visitors were due to arrive at 11AM and at 10.40 I was at the front door of the bank, just outside the huge reception area and surrounded by two or three of our security staff along with Mr Alan Trebbish. Suddenly, three black Rolls Royces slid to a halt in front of the building and around ten people got out, each wearing almost identical black suits. They were serious and unsmiling. I stepped forward to greet whom I thought was the most senior man. As I approached, three of his colleagues grasped my arms and pulled me back. My colleagues looked on in horror. I realised pretty quickly that these good folk were not remotely Chinese, particularly since one of them shouted, "*Ottengali via da me schiuma!*" Now I do know some Italian and I also know when Italian isn't Chinese and further do I know that what this gentleman said was, "Get away from me you scum!" Not nice eh?

There was more scuffling and apologies from our side that something may be amiss. Soon the ten gangster-looking types were bustled into the building whereupon the main man shouted, "*Ciò non è l'italiano dichiara la banca! Andiamo! Questa gente è idiots!*" ("This isn't the Italian State Bank! Let's go! These people are idiots!") Unfortunately, or fortunately, Mrs Sourdough was passing at the time and the gangster had the sense to bow apologetically, after which all ten rushed out, knocking over Mr Alan Trebbish in the process.

Helping the not-so-young Mr Alan Trebbish to his feet, I breathed a sigh of some relief, but that was short-lived by a squawking mobile phone… mine. "Where the hell are you Arfur?" shouted Jez Staffordshire. "There are fifteen Chinese genmun standing in a circle rahnd your desk! If this is the delegation for Sir Christopher you might want to a) leave the country or b) get here right now!"

Well, you can guess the rest. The Chinese delegation had obviously been misdirected into the building. They were perfectly calm and patient and were talking quietly amongst themselves. One was looking curiously at Jenny who was practising her Lady Macduff and some of her ballet routines. I introduced myself, managed the card handovers pretty smartly, bowed in all the right places, said, "受欢迎的先生们。非常喜悦遇见您。" which (roughly) means, "Welcome gentlemen. Very pleased to meet you." They all smiled and then, to my horror, clapped. I asked them to follow me and led them with grace and precision, single file, to the lift and thence to the 41st floor, although I had to ask everyone in the lift to kindly leave since I had an important delegation to meet Sir Christopher. My tone of authority (or sheer panic) must have been sufficient, because everyone did as I told them so to do. When I handed my charges over to Sir Christopher's people, there was some confusion on people's faces but all was well.

Mr Bose was pleased with me.

Regards

Arthur

57

From: Arthur Shilling [arthur.shilling@gammondhopes.com]
Sent: 04/20/2012 21.16 PM GMT
To: Steven Charteris [stevencharteris@staracademy.com]
Subject: The Orient calls and I have read some Omar Khayyam

Steven

Mary Haringey visited me last weekend. You'll remember her. She was in my second year Dickens' seminar group. You know, eyes going in two directions. She's doing very well, has had the squint fixed and is now a cub journalist with a well-known broadsheet. She said that she'd heard that Mrs C had been in a spot of further bother with the police, but I refused to entertain that line of conversation or give any particulars – not that I know any. She likes quoting Dickens at me and we had a two-hour dialogue made up of as much Victorian street language as we could recall. I won.

Hong Kong beckons and I've nearly completed Mr F's two speeches. One of them Mr Bose wanted me to show Zalautha Derong because part of it involved West African trade and Zalautha hails from that part of the world and is, I understand, a specialist in West African economics. She wanted a hard copy so that she could mark it up. I agreed and within an hour a copy was on her desk. I received her red-marked comments by the end of the day, but I truly couldn't read a word. Not only that, there were bits of potato crisps all over the document and smudges of what I deduced to be cheese or, what I can only hope was, chutney. I threw the lot in the green 'paper to be recycled' bin and said to Zalautha that, while her comments had been erudite and straightforward, I'd really appreciate a discussion with her to establish exactly what she had meant. She seemed reasonably flattered and, although there was some initial confusion as I explained why her marked-up copy was in the bin, that's what we did. Derek Rattles interrupted saying that Dephne Hong might have to miss part of the Chairman's Strategic Forum in Hong Kong due to a family illness and, if that was indeed the case, then I would have to step up to the plate and manage. He smiled toothily and departed. I couldn't concentrate much on Zalautha after that.

Samarkand, I have just discovered, is nowhere near Hong Kong.

Regards to you and, of course, to dear Mrs C

Arthur

58

From: Arthur Shilling [arthur.shilling@gammondhopes.com]
Sent: 04/27/2012 23.16 PM GMT
To: Steven Charteris [stevencharteris@staracademy.com]
Subject: Hong Kong

Dear Steven

Take it that I have bowed to you in greeting you this evening.
你好 (Hello) or 你好吗? (How are you?)

Hong Kong is extraordinary. It's as if some mighty warrior of the ancients had deposited a modern city right in the middle of a mountain range. The approach by air is fantastic and once I was through passport control I was welcomed by a liveried chauffeur who whisked me off to our hotel where the conference is to be held. It's right smack in the commercial quarter and everything is lit up.

As I mentioned, Dephne Hong is otherwise engaged and can't be with us on this leg of the event, so it's down to me. The event producer is Raspberry Jenkins once again and we now work well as a team. She has a good crew (mostly Welsh!), although the local technicians are never around when she wants them and the hotel staff are often AWOL as well. But, by and large, we're managing.

I've rewritten the Chairman's address because this time it's Sir Christopher who will open and close the event. He doesn't care for bullet points and I have to type the whole thing word for word. At least he's stopped calling me the wrong name and now just says 'you'. Unfortunately when he says 'you', everyone turns as one, not knowing to which 'you' he is referring.

There are some local bank dignitaries I need to meet in order to establish whether one of them should speak at the first evening's dinner… or all eight! I am plumping for the former, but I'm told that protocol might insist on the latter – which will totally mess up the running order and cause mayhem in the already rattled hotel kitchens.

Sir Christopher is here early on business and he popped in to see how things were going. As a joke one of the crew had put the company's logo on the set's backdrop upside down. Sir C wasn't particularly amused and I suppose neither was anyone else. We were obliged to rectify the matter while he waited and there was a frosty atmosphere as he eyed me with some hostility. However, when he asked to see his speech and I had a freshly printed copy to hand, he looked at me with appreciation (I like to think). He needs to consume some mints.

When I got to the event production office – a small room near the auditorium stuffed full of boxes with handouts, brochures, local maps, badges and so on – I worked on my emails for about an hour or so. Being in charge means I have to check and see that there are no cancellations or contributors who've decided not to turn up at the last moment. There was an odd email from a senior manager in Mexico. The English was very strange and I was struggling to make sense of it: "I see you tomorrow and then unfortunate accident. I go upstair and knock on door with the jelly. They call doctor and soon a young locust attend me. Married twelve year but no chill yet. Yesterday refuse give evidence to police and charge with assault and carrying a gnu. Please apologise." And more in similar vein. I boggled at the thought of what the poor woman had gone through particularly if a 'gnu' was really a gun, but then was quickly brought back to the here and now by our gentle producer rushing in and saying that the banqueting manager wanted to see me urgently. I nodded and did as I was bid (or is it bidden?).

The banqueting manager, a rake-thin, short lady of middle years with scraped-back jet black hair and a smart pin-stripe suit, was beside herself with anger. Apparently, Sir Christopher had asked to see the menu for the first evening's dinner and had vetoed most of the dishes. When asked what he wanted instead, he just said "something a little more appetising, if you don't mind." So I now had to spend the next two hours pacifying chefs and other assorted hotel staff in the construction of another menu. Having managed that, the producer wanted me to run through all the PowerPoint presentations, during the course of which I espied Mr Goodenhardt fast asleep on two chairs at the back of the room with a copy of *Macbeth* in his hand. Curious. Despite the fact that drool was slipping gently from the corner of his mouth, I decided to leave him alone.

I am of the opinion that Mrs Goodenhardt is trying to emulate Lady Macbeth in plotting to do away with Mr Flattergleich!

Regards in haste

Arthur

59

From: Arthur Shilling [arthur.shilling@gammondhopes.com]
Sent: 04/28/2012 19.16 PM GMT
To: Steven Charteris [stevencharteris@staracademy.com]
Subject: Still Hong Kong, but the Orient is jolly hard work

Steven

All's gone very well so far, apart from the first evening's dinner when the local dignitaries complained (privately of course) about the menu and the fact that all eight weren't allowed to speak. Sir C was oblivious and was reported to have been heartily tucking into his beef. The vegetarian options should have been superb but weren't, and someone from Basingstoke (a very large lady with huge bunions encased in tiny silver slippers) decided that her supper wasn't properly vegan after all. Mr Bose, as ever, went to have a word and, while I really don't know what it is he says to people in times of high stress, the large lady subsided, nodded a great deal, cried a little, rested her head upon his shoulder for a moment, nodded again and indeed magically stopped making a fuss. And ate everything on her plate. Even when Sir C was looking round for someone to yell at because he'd left his script in his room, Mr Bose noiselessly stepped up with another copy. How he does these things I have no idea. I looked out for him later to offer thanks, but of the great man there was no sight.

Today, delegates are discussing several topics, including the perennial 'Winners and losers: what will economies, governments and corporations have gained and lost by 2030?', which went down well in Dubai and at which we have the Chairman of a well known oil and gas company addressing us, together with a former editor of an equally well known international business magazine.

Mr Derek Rattles has been asked to address the event on a topic devised by him – 'changing communication tools'. I offered to help with this one, but he has insisted that he "fly solo thank you Arthur Shilling – I have actually done these things before you know", as he put it. He is determined to use no PowerPoint. Mr Rattles has just gone up in my estimation by 100% despite being something of a plonker sometimes. Yes I know – offer respect to my betters – but I'm saying this to you as a brother in arms. Great *Dire Straits* album by the way. I know that Mrs C used to be keen back in the day.

The Hong Kong event has been facilitated by a CNN big cheese and, while he's a touch brash, he certainly moves the event along at a decent pace. He's good with Q&A sessions too, although he sometimes doesn't let the microphone reach the questioner – so we get that rather annoying scenario when someone mumbles and then suddenly booms the latter half of a question which, of course, nobody then understands. There was a session on the topic: 'Can large international companies please enough people enough of the time?', to which Sir Christopher said gruffly and creakily, "Yes, of course," and turned away to pour a glass of water which, because his levalier microphone was so close to the carafe, sounded as if a large horse was relieving itself in the auditorium.

Our Hong Kong host, the bank's regional GM, has been very kind to me and has suggested that I return one day to enjoy his great country. Despite the fact that his family tales are all-encompassing in making one go instantly to sleep, I have readily agreed (with genuine enthusiasm) and feel like an international banker already. When we left, he shook my hand for an age and wouldn't let it go. I patted him on the shoulder and tried to leave, but he and I ended up doing something of a hand jive. The Americans among our team, including Mr Goodenhardt, shook hands with our hosts as if they were pumping up airbeds.

Back to the real world, alas. But in business class – yey!

As ever,

Arthur

60

From: Arthur Shilling [arthur.shilling@gammondhopes.com]
Sent: 05/04/2012 23.16 PM GMT
To: Steven Charteris [stevencharteris@staracademy.com]
Subject: Zalautha Derong

Steven

Back home and my landlady, dear Victoria Holyhead with the fabulous red hair, was moderately pleased with the the Chinese *choujiu* (made from glutinous rice) that I brought back for her. She looked at the bottle, smiled at me in a fixed sort of way and went off to make false boils or warts or something.

I've posted a bottle of snake wine for Mrs C which is meant to have all kinds of healing powers. I know that it's alcoholic but a small draught now and again shouldn't hurt. The drink was first recorded to have been consumed in China during the Western Zhou dynasty and was believed to be a cure-all. Snake wine is an alcoholic beverage produced by infusing whole snakes in rice wine. The snakes used, preferably venomous ones so I'm told, have their venom dissolved in the liquor.

Zalautha Derong is leaving. She is being posted to Mozambique and is not at all happy about the move. However, it is an (almost) unwritten rule within the bank that if you're offered a promotion, no matter where it is, it's professional suicide to refuse, particularly if you're an international manager or in the bank's fast lane. Poor Z has been crying on and off all week and everyone is in two minds as to whether they should offer comfort or congratulations. When I offered commiserations tinged with a hearty toast in the form of a raised cup of cooling coffee, she'd been crying (again) and she'd also been comforting herself with a good round or two of cheese and chutney sandwiches, as a consequence of which I was sprayed with half-eaten substance. I tried hard not to wince or recoil in an overly adverse way.

Jenny Barstiff and Mrs Sourdough have taken it upon themselves to organise a leaving party for Z – which I'm much looking forward to because lovely Chloe from PR is going!

Macbeth is moving forward nicely, although the three witches are comprised of two ladies from catering and an effeminate young actuary. They are definitely *not* a cohesive unit and, despite the encouragement from our director, Ms Nookles (who looks leaner and more exhausted by the week), they don't seem to be a) in charge of their lines or b) remotely threatening. Jenny Barstiff is becoming very impatient and I've had to hold her back indicating that she can't really play Lady Macduff and a witch. The director agrees. Jenny just rants and tells everyone in the production that, because Lady Macduff is the wife of Macduff, the Thane of Fife, *and* the mother of an unnamed son and other children, it would be perfectly acceptable if she, Jenny, was a witch as well. Jenny says that her appearance in the play as Lady Macduff is brief: she and her son are introduced in Act IV Scene ii, a climactic and tragic scene that ends with the loss of both her and her son's life, so nobody in the audience would recognise her as a witch. The director is adamant, so Jenny has now resorted to telling us that, although Lady Macduff's appearance is limited to the death scene and not a lot else, her role in the play is hugely significant. She now plans to makes the death scene last for a full five minutes.

I was called in to see Mr Flattergleich about his future speech commitments. He's concerned about body language and wants everyone in the department to be able to advise internal clients on the dos and don'ts in the field of body language. He is convinced that we are not properly versed in the topic and, as he put it, "Being an international organisation, we neet to be verr clear about giving off poor signals." I'm not quite sure what I have to do and Mr F doesn't yet have a plan. He just wants a few of us to consider what should be done.

I had rather a severe email from our top chap in Singapore who claims that I was somewhat insulting when his senior staff and I had gone out for dinner in HK. I was accompanied by an Englishman who worked in the HK office but who was of no help at all in ensuring the evening's success. He used to be a publisher and was even less successful at that profession. The bill for the dinner had been horrendous and I had to spend the best part of 40 minutes figuring out who should pay for what. I didn't realise that this was a local faux pas and, indeed, nobody thought to point it out, particularly the local colleague who's an idiot. Needless to say, I responded to the email with utmost and abject apologies and an offer to put the matter right when I returned one day. I received no reply although Mr Rattles, to whom the original email had been copied, did have a quiet word, so quiet in fact that I couldn't catch all that he said – although I did get the drift.

Arthur

>

From: Steven Charteris [stevencharteris@staracademy.com]
Sent: 05/10/2012 10.16 AM GMT
To: Arthur Shilling [arthur.shilling@gammondhopes.com]
Subject: "There's daggers in men's smiles"

Dear Arthur

Recognise the quote above? Of course you do. *Macbeth* is clearly absorbing your time. Let it not become overpowering.

Hong Kong is interesting. When I was in corporate life, I spent much time there. In terms of the general Hong Kong work environment, the place is regarded as a gateway into the Chinese market.

Doing business in China

- Much Chinese business is contracted in Hong Kong. While fulfilment takes place largely in the hinterland, financial services is still HK's mainstay. Many multinational and local companies have their head office there and yours I know is pretty huge. Manufacturing and back-office functions tend to be located over the border in places like Shenzhen (a city with 'Special Economic Zone' status I believe).

- If you are conducting business in China, it's worth doing some homework. Your company will likely send you on a language course or two. As you'll have discovered, although English is usually spoken in HK, most local staff communicate with each other in Cantonese and there are some cultural sensitivities to be mindful of. Examples include the giving and receiving of business cards with both hands and paying for staff when entertaining socially. Unlike in the West, the bill is not divided and the boss always pays.

Body language

- The success of any encounter begins the moment someone meets you. Your appearance says something about you long before you open your mouth. One of the first key things people notice is how you carry and present yourself. Do you walk and stand with confidence?

- Another vital component to any interpersonal encounter is a firm handshake – those few seconds can empower or weaken a relationship. Ingredients of a good handshake: hold the person's hand firmly, shake three times maximum, maintain constant eye contact and smile.

- Eye contact is important. Not only does it display confidence on your part, it also helps you understand what the other person is really saying. Ralph Waldo Emerson said, "When the eyes say one thing, and the tongue another, a practiced man relies on the language of the first." Looking someone in the eye as you talk also shows that you are paying attention.

- Listening is the most important human relations skill and good eye contact plays a large part in conveying our interest in others. Be sure to maintain direct eye contact as you say goodbye. It will help leave a lasting, positive impression.

- Not looking at someone while he or she is talking can be interpreted as discomfort, evasiveness, a lack of confidence or boredom. On the other hand, staring can be construed as being too direct, dominant or forceful and might make the other person uncomfortable. Avoid looking over the other person's shoulders as if you were seeking out someone more interesting to talk with.

- Smiles are important – they show interest, excitement, empathy and concern. If you enter a meeting which has already started, smile at the leader or chair and acknowledge others as they catch your eye or you theirs.

- Mrs C once complained that, over an academic luncheon in Florence years ago, all the Italians were shouting at and talking over each other. She thought that they were about to have a fight! But this is just normal everyday communication in Italy. Mind you, when she wandered across a busy road without first looking left or right, a policeman did shout at her and she, thinking by then that this was just everyday parlance, merely waved back.

Cultural differences
- The biggest cultural differences exist mainly in relation to territorial space, eye contact, touch frequency and insult gestures. The regions that have the greatest number of different local signals are Arab countries as well as parts of Asia and Japan. Understanding cultural differences is too big a subject to be covered in one email (and, besides which, I'm

not an expert) so we'll stick to the basic things that you are likely to see abroad.

— When it comes to greeting with a kiss on the cheek, the Scandinavians are happy with a single kiss, the French prefer a double, while the Dutch, Belgians and Arabs go for a triple. The Brits either avoid kissing by standing back or will surprise you with a European double kiss. The Australians, New Zealanders and Americans are continually confused about greeting kisses and bump noses as they fumble their way through a single peck.

— Handshakes, kissing and hugs are not the norm in Japan, where such contact is considered impolite. The Japanese bow and exchange business cards on first meeting; the person with the highest status bowing the least and the one with the least status bowing the most. In Japan, make sure your shoes are clean and in good condition. Every time a Japanese person bows, he or she (allegedly) inspects them. Mrs C learnt a harsh lesson when she was caught in a Shizuoka thunderstorm and her best shoes were caked in mud.

— The head nod is an almost universal sign for 'yes', except for the Bulgarians who use the gesture to signify 'no' and the Japanese who use it for politeness. If you say something with which a Japanese person doesn't agree, he or she will still say 'yes' – or *hai* in Japanese. In India, shaking one's head can mean agreement or 'yes'.

— In places that have strong British influence, such as Australia, the USA, South Africa, Singapore and New Zealand, the thumbs-up gesture has a few meanings: it's a signal implying that all's well but when the thumb is jerked sharply upwards it can become an insult. In some countries such as Greece, the thumb is thrust forward and it mainly means 'get stuffed'.

I must finish this shortly for I note the hour and my cooling cauliflower and pasta cheese dish for one will shortly be dustbin material. Oh yes, another thing – touching is a minefield. Whether or not someone will be offended by touch during conversation depends on their culture. Mrs Agnew, who cleans our modest home twice a week, has no problems with invading space or touching. That would be fine, but the alcohol on her breath suffused with an odour of snuff makes the encounter difficult and, in the case of Mrs C, disastrous. The French and Italians love to continually touch as they talk, while the British prefer not to touch at any time unless it's on a sports field in front of a large audience and a goal or race has been scored or won. Touching is fine (within reason of course as Mrs C now knows) in India, Turkey, France, Italy, Greece, Spain, the Middle East, parts of Asia and Russia.

Ultimately, people do business with people who make them feel comfortable and this comes down to sincerity and good manners.

I must run now. Sorry that your cheese-and-onion-crisp-eating lady colleague is leaving. Keep in touch and call her from time to time. Good friends are scarce and, if indeed she is one (although you don't really say), then they are worth cultivating. Don't rely on the other person to make the effort.

Regards

Charteris

Chapter Seven

"If music be the food of love, play on,
Give me excess of it; that surfeiting,
The appetite may sicken, and so die."

Duke Orsino: *Twelfth Night* (I, i)

61

From: Arthur Shilling [arthur.shilling@gammondhopes.com]
Sent: 05/16/2012 23.16 PM GMT
To: Steven Charteris [stevencharteris@staracademy.com]
Subject: Black tights

Steven

I saw a TV programme on drug addiction a week or so ago and there are many new treatments available (particularly, and oddly enough, in Rumania) for those who might be regarded as dope fiends – not, of course, that your good lady is a dope fiend – but I thought you might be interested.

I still don't really understand dear old Mr Bose. Well, he's not actually old of course, but extraordinarily wise certainly. I have to say that he has really been a tower of strength and, to date, he has always found time to give me help when needed and sometimes when not – despite his own heavy workload.

Today Mr Almoun sprang a surprise and insisted that we all attend an impromptu role-playing presentation. It was an after work occasion and everyone was a bit jaded at that, particularly Mrs Sourdough who said that weekdays were difficult. She didn't explain, so we all wondered why. I shall be late for a rehearsal.

In the conference theatre, Mr Almoun introduced the importance of understanding useful techniques for considering difficult situations before they occur. He said that there had been too many examples of certain situations getting out of hand. Everyone glanced at Mr Goodenhardt and then Jenny Barstiff, neither of whom looked remotely embarrassed. Everyone glanced not so discreetly at one another and there were a few red faces amongst the congregation. Mr Almoun then leapt about on the stage lit up by a follow spot, the operator of which was trying desperately to keep him fixed. "Role-play," Mr A shouted, "can be used to analyse problems from different perspectives to help teamwork. Remember teamwork people? Eh? Teamwork? Team… Work… Works!" I thought that he was about to break into song.

We were then introduced to three 'educational actors' – two men and a buxom woman, all dressed in black with tights that were eye-wateringly constricting. The leader of the black tights was a rotund gent who seemingly wanted to address the ceiling and who said something like, "Ladies and ahhh gentlemeeeen. By acting the scenarios through, participants (you good people) can pre-experience the likely reactions to different approaches and can get a feel for the approaches that will work and those that might be counter-productive. Catch me drift? And by repeating the scenarios, people can understand how different approaches might work, so that an ideal approach can be identified. Catch me drift now? More than this, by preparing for a situation using role-play, people build up experience and self-confidence in handling the situation in real life. You good people will instinctively correct reactions to situations, meaning that you can react effectively as situations evolve rather than making mistakes or being overwhelmed by events. Catch me very drift? I thank you." Everyone was agape and agog.

The three then demonstrated a number of interactions: angry customer with stupid receptionist, angry customer with bright receptionist, angry banker with angry other banker, angry customer with happy plumber and so on. Then we had to take similar roles and work in twos or threes to achieve some sort of therapeutic resolution, during which Mr Almoun leapt about some more, sticking his glistening head in amongst the groups and occasionally winking at a number of us.

Finally, and after much harsh staring at watches and clocks, the rotund one, now with tights seemingly even tighter around his nether regions, blew a whistle and called a halt. "Next week, everyone, we'll get a number of you up on stage to explore some of your excellent improvisations." Mr Bose looked hard at him then at Mr Almoun who, in turn, looked somewhat abashed if only for a microsecond. Then, we all trooped off – all of us somewhat bereft of conversation.

Best to the Charteris household

Arthur

62

From: Arthur Shilling [arthur.shilling@gammondhopes.com]
Sent: 05/20/2012 23.16 PM GMT
To: Steven Charteris [stevencharteris@staracademy.com]
Subject: The Scottish play

Dear Steven

Last night was the first of *Macbeth* but, alas, it was not the success that everyone had hoped it would be. For starters, the cues were all over the place and people kept coming in and exiting at all the wrong points, causing mayhem to the sense and content. I acquitted myself reasonably and, in fact, our producer said of my performance that "you, Arthur, have acquitted yourself reasonably well", although she may perhaps have said "tolerably" instead of "reasonably". For the ghost scene, my costume was highlighted in luminous paint but, rather than creating a ghostly effect, it created a pantomime skeletal figure and the audience, thinking this to be a comic moment (Philistines!) just fell about with pathetic laughter – so much so that Macbeth and those around the stage dining table couldn't make themselves heard and, indeed, they too were trying hard not to laugh. I could distinctly see Jez Staffordshire on the front row helpless with mirth – unfair I thought, considering how much I helped him from total embarrassment in Wales.

I am to take responsibility for a number of TV interviews that our Deputy Chairman is undertaking. I have to liaise with the broadcast people and handle all the logistics and make life easy for our new TV star-to-be. As I have mentioned, Sir Christopher has a voice like a rusty gate. If modulated or tutored he could, I think, sound like Alan Rickman in the *Harry Potter* films, but nobody is ever going to suggest that he (Sir C not Mr R) should have speech training. Mr Bose has given me a few tips on TV interviews and how to deal with the media, but I wasn't listening since Jenny Barstiff was, at the time, performing the *Dance of the Seven Veils* behind his back and it was distracting in all sorts of ways.

I *do* keep wondering whether Mrs C would benefit from a visit to Rumania and a drug dependency health programme. What do you think? I have the details before me and the facilities do look first class! You could go for a vacation.

Best, as ever

Arthur Shilling

63

From: Arthur Shilling [arthur.shilling@gammondhopes.com]
Sent:05/25/2012 20.16 PM GMT
To: Steven Charteris [stevencharteris@staracademy.com]
Subject: TV people

Steven

Yesterday was the first day's shoot for the TV interviews. The interview was recorded of course and apparently they're all to be edited later. Sir Christopher asked me *en passant* if the bank had editorial control over output and I, not knowing what he was talking about, said yes and beamed helpfully. He looked at me and then nodded. "Very good," he said. "Make sure that you take Rattles or Flattergleich or, better still, Bose with you." Again, not knowing what he was talking about, I nodded and trotted off to the TV producer's side. They drink an awful lot of tea and coffee, these television folk, and insist on sausage sandwiches and iced buns.

The television people were decent enough. There was a discussion about where the interview might take place, with the programme director (a middle-aged gent wearing a flat cap and a flowing blue silk scarf plus very tight jeans and an even tighter T-shirt with 'Holy Moly' writ large on the front) refusing to accept any intervention from me or indeed Sir Christopher's PA. Eventually they all agreed that the Chairman's office would be best and that was fine, since our master was in the United States at the time.

They are going to produce three 15-minute programmes, each of which will detail a particular aspect of the bank's expertise. The first is to be about South America and burgeoning markets (particularly Mexico), the second about people and the third on the topic of world trade.

Mr Bose is on leave or somewhere at the moment, so I can't discuss anything with him. Mr Flattergleich wasn't much help because he'd done little in the way of TV and media interviews. And Jez is busy with something VERY IMPORTANT as he keeps indicating in his emails.

Regards to the effervescent Mrs C and, of course, to you

Arthur

64

From: Arthur Shilling [arthur.shilling@gammondhopes.com]
Sent: 06/05/2012 20.16 PM GMT
To: Steven Charteris [stevencharteris@staracademy.com]
Subject: TV chaos

Dear Steven

Chaos is come. Doomed. The first of the TV programmes has been aired – perhaps you saw it – nine o'clock last night. It was all about Mexico. Needless to say, the bank had no editorial control whatsoever over the content or delivery of any of the programmes.

You'd have thought that Mexico was quite a safe subject. Well, ha ha. The production company set the programme in the city of Nogales, just twelve miles from the US border on a known smuggling route. The setting was in the middle of local elections and it seemed that the bank's activities – presented as criminal – overshadowed everything else. Sir Christopher's comments were made into a voiceover for the most part and he sounded like a very posh, corroded gate. Viewers might have thought that he was a British overlord of a huge drug dealing ring! The producers made out that the bank had sponsored a fresh wave of drug-related violence including, for goodness' sake, a full-scale gunfight between rival gangs in which 29 people were alleged to have been shot or wounded. The so-called 'narcoelecciones', widely seen as a referendum on the President's anti-drugs crusade, were directly affected by the violence – violence sponsored (so the programme suggested) by our bank! People are going round the office today calling Sir Christopher El Cid and me Zorro although I do believe that they have their history totally confused. As if that wasn't enough, the Mexican opposition party, the PRI, has sent an email to our PR department demanding a seat on the GH Board. I have been summoned to a meeting with Mr Flattergleich and Sir Christopher's senior advisers.

I might be writing my next missive from prison or the gutter. The only consolation is that my beautiful red-haired make up artist landlady, Victoria, laughed like a drain and gave me a hug saying that I should join the BBC and make comedy programmes. The hug keeps me sane Steven, as does your friendship. Try as I might, I cannot "Give sorrow words. The grief that does not speak whispers the o'er-fraught heart, and bids it break."

Arthur

65

From: Arthur Shilling [arthur.shilling@gammondhopes.com]
Sent: 06/15/2012 19.16 PM GMT
To: Steven Charteris [stevencharteris@staracademy.com]
Subject: TV should be banned

Steven

The TV crisis became worse of course. The programme on the bank's staff made everyone look like zombies or idiots or both. Zombies are the new vampires of course, but that's little consolation for a programme on current business practice. Mind you, Brad Pitt, Marc Forster and the producers of *World War Z* might have learnt a thing or two. Sir Christopher's grating voice now makes him sound like a Victorian English squire who employs serfs and pays them in beetroot and old sacks. Jez and

Mr Almoun think its hugely funny and congratulated me on my verve and initiative in establishing a new style of reportage. I tried to explain that the resulting programmes had nothing to do with me, but they just clasped me to their bosoms and laughed all the more. They both shook my hand and wished me good fortune for the future, convinced as they are that my Grammond Hopes career would be cut short imminently.

The third programme was no better. This was on world trade and we were made to look like a bunch of pirates. The 15 minutes seemed to go on forever. I watched it with my red-haired landlady and she laughed again like a drain, saying that this would probably win a comedy prize at the next BAFTA awards. The piece even featured a snippet from one of *The Pirates of the Caribbean* movies! I don't see Sir Christopher as Johnny Depp really.

When people in the corridors or lifts see me, they snigger or, in the case of one of the technical support people in the company's auditorium, well he just held my shoulders with both hands and laughed as real tears rolled down his ruddy cheeks. I thought he was about to have apoplexy.

But in the midst of this chaos, there was a glimmer of hope. Mr Flattergleich is hosting a banking conference that the UK Prime Minister will be attending and I'm to have nothing to do with it! Phew! Mind you, it could of course be that I won't be allowed *any* contact with *anything* of any importance before I leave the company, which will undoubtedly be soon.

Despondently yours

Arthur

66

From: Arthur Shilling [arthur.shilling@gammondhopes.com]
Sent: 06/21/2012 23.16 PM GMT
To: Steven Charteris [stevencharteris@staracademy.com]
Subject: Aye me

Dear Steven

I do recall once you saying that all is not as bleak as it might seem. Well, it jolly well is. I had a meeting with Sir Christopher's people along with my departmental seniors and betters. I didn't get much of a chance to say anything. Everyone just gesticulated wildly and threw newspaper cuttings in my direction. Chloe from PR was there and, while she threw nothing in my direction apart from a wry smile, she said nothing at all in my defence. Mr Bose wasn't present.

When the meeting ended, I was left alone and it was a bit like one of those old films when the chap's left in his room with one bullet in his gun and a bottle of whiskey. There's an audition next week for *Twelfth Night* but I don't feel much like going – not much point if I won't be in the bank. Shame really because I fancied myself as a good Sir Andrew Aguecheek. Do you remember my Malvolio? Not bad I think. My comedic side needs an airing, although my levels of current comedy are at an all time low. You always said my Fool from *King Lear* was good, although a tad over the top.

In the depths of despond,

Arthur

67

From: Arthur Shilling [arthur.shilling@gammondhopes.com]
Sent: 06/22/2012 22.16 PM GMT
To: Steven Charteris [stevencharteris@staracademy.com]
Subject: Extraordinary!

Dearest Steven (if I might be so bold)

The most amazing thing has happened! I'm suddenly the golden boy! I even got a kiss from Mrs Sourdough and she actually tried some Shakespeare: "If music be the food of love, I'd 'ave a slice of you Mr Shilling." Well it's a start. One of the national newspapers has run a series of articles on the bravery of this bank to present itself in a *real* way (their italics). The articles waxed lyrical about how the bank had the guts to talk honestly and openly about major issues in the world today and, in particular, the sensitive manner in which we manage our international business. I was asked to go to see Sir Christopher who, when I did, shook my hand, called me Brian Smiling and thanked me for my input. When I returned to my desk, Mr Bose caught my eye and he smiled a smile which made me think that he might have a hand in this turnaround of affairs.

Jez and Mr Almoun had the grace to come over and clasp me to their substantial bosoms again with, I suspect, some dismay in their visages. Chloe had the decency to visit too, with rather too much gushing congratulations for my taste. She told me though that all PR contacts with the media have to go through her now and that I should have nothing to do with TV people or PR folk. Fine by me. I shrugged a shrug of the famous. She frowned the frown of an irritated PR executive, turned on her expensive Jimmy Choo heels and walked off, flicking her hair over a gorgeous shoulder as she went. Do you know how much Jimmy Choos *are*?

Anyway, I will now audition for Sir Andrew – it's the least I can do. Unfortunately, the play's being done in modern dress. I do hope that I won't be too critical of whoever plays Malvolio – a part, as you know, that I do regard as my own. Almost, dare I say, as good as my Mercutio which was, people said, historic.

But this evening, I'm out on the town and will be going for a few beers with some colleagues including best bud Graham Graveling who is going to try for Olivia (don't ask). I would ask Chloe to come for a drink too, but I'm not sure of my grounds although I am becoming rather fond. I've had an email from Mr Flattergleich expressing relief that all's seemingly well, although he says that a large number of corporate shareholders are still less than happy. As they say in show biz, you just can't win 'em all. Perhaps they don't say that, but you know what I mean.

Huge relief.

Regards

Arthur Shilling

P.S. I think that I might be related to John Charles Walsham Reith, 1st Baron Reith and also first DG of the BBC. Maybe that's where I get my flair for TV!

68

From: Arthur Shilling [arthur.shilling@gammondhopes.com]
Sent: 06/27/2012 06.16 AM GMT
To: Steven Charteris [stevencharteris@staracademy.com]
Subject: Germany

Steven

Mr Flattergleich is going to Germany and I am to go with him to assist with scripts. It's only a three-day visit but I've not been to Germany since my school exchange trip – which was disastrous, since the family to which I was sent, in Auerbach in der Oberpfalz, was strict Lutheran and the spartan lifestyle and discipline have probably scarred me for life.

Mr F and I are to visit Berlin and Freiburg im Breisgau. Berlin is an important centre for the bank and Freiburg is an excellent example of sustainability – Mr F is producing a speech on the bank's sustainability mission. He's using Freiburg as an example, not least because we have apparently helped fund some of the Freiburg developments. Eco housing, car-free streets and socially conscious neighbours have made the German city a shining example of sustainability, says Mr F.

Mr Bose still uses his unending supply of pristine pencils as drum sticks and we all now know when he's deepest in thought – when his drumming reaches a level of which Charlie Watts would be proud. The drumming is always very impressive and on a number of occasions Jenny Barstiff has walked by Mr B's desk and has suddenly crouched low, clicking her fingers and tried to sing a small selection from *West Side Story*.

I was telephoned by a nasty chap who called himself Jim Buddleia (or so it sounded); he claims to be a marketing expert who wants to find me a publisher for my new book. "What new book?" I asked. "The one I'm going to help you publish, Mr Shilling," was the sneering reply. "The one that explains how you made a bank famous." His voice was slimy and I took an instant dislike to the fellow. "I don't want to write a book, thank you," I replied curtly and put down the phone. Later, much later, I wondered whether I had made the right decision.

Regards

Literati one and all

Arthur

P.S. I am no relation to The Lord Reith, so stand easy. But, as Marlon Brando said in one of my favourite films, *On the Waterfront*, "I coulda had class. I coulda been a contender. I coulda been somebody, instead of a bum, which is what I am, let's face it. It was you, Charley." On second thoughts the scenarios aren't quite the same but you'll accept my point no doubt. Also, I don't know anyone called Charley.

69

From: Arthur Shilling [arthur.shilling@gammondhopes.com]
Sent: 07/03/2012 07.16 AM GMT
To: Steven Charteris [stevencharteris@staracademy.com]
Subject: Our German friends

Well, Steven

Germany is *wunderbar und Einfach nur genial* (wonderful and simply brilliant). I can't recall how your German is, so I'll try not to confuse, although I'm thinking in German now of course and my sentence construction – *satzbau* – he tends to be the out of window going.

Berlin was terrific, really. Our five-star hotel – magic. The local team headed by Herr Willy Hoffman, a rotund and jovial fellow of middle years, looked after us splendidly. Willy had a tendency to begin every sentence with a "Ho, zen, now", which was fine but a little jarring because the end of each sentence tended to finish with a hearty "*Ja. ist das in Ordnung? Lassen Sie uns jetzt gehen.*" which means "Yes. Is that ok? Let us to do it." But he was a decent enough chap and he entertained us royally. I have *never* eaten so much.

The evening we arrived we went with Herr Hoffman and his round wife Helga to a medieval-themed restaurant. Accompanying the party were two of Herr Hoffman's colleagues (Hans Schulz and Hans Bauer) plus their wives. That was fine, but made it a tad hard for both Mr F and myself who had no wives with us and, in my case, none anywhere. The two gents called Hans caused some difficulty and no mirth whatsoever, so we had to keep pleasantries fairly formal. Their English was superb and their accents far better than Mr F's, although he didn't seem to mind, so happy was he to be in his homeland and his own city. The medieval Fool kept jangling his bells in my face until I was obliged to stop his hand at one point and broke his jester's stick in half. I concentrated on the ladies at our table since nobody else was, but was only treated to a gentle '*ja*' or '*nein*' or a sigh to my various questions about a) children, b) education, c) cars (just happened), d) politics and e) food, particularly chicken done in a kind of creamy lemon sauce (or '*sose*' as it was described by one of the Hans ladies).

Food seemed to be the ladies' favourite subject. "*Hat Ihnen der Hering?*" asked one. Not wanting them to think I hadn't understood, I replied, "The pickled herring was substantial", which received a blank look from Mrs Bauer. "Delicious," I said loudly and rubbed my tummy enthusiastically. She beamed and said, with smiles galore and smudged lipstick, "*Dann müssen Sie versuchen, etwas von diesem Schaf das Verdauungssystem. Es ist wirklich sehr lecker.*" I protested that I was full. The idea of eating a sheep's digestive system, no matter how interestingly served, filled me with no small horror. Mrs Schulz, a small and fiery woman, piped up with, "*Aber Sie werden die Torte mit Kirsch und Ananas Blüte Schnaps probieren?*" I had to agree, although the last thing I wanted at that moment was a slab of kirsch-flavoured cake suffused with pineapple blossom brandy. I did my duty of course. Meanwhile the gentlemen of the party excluded me totally from their cheerful business banter. I hadn't seen Mr F so content.

Tomorrow Freiburg.

Best wishes

Artur (I consider this a much better spelling – it has something of Wagner about it)

70

From: Arthur Shilling [arthur.shilling@gammondhopes.com]
Sent: 07/05/2012 09.16 AM GMT
To: Steven Charteris [stevencharteris@staracademy.com]
Subject: The Black Forest and its Cremetörtchen

Herr Professor Charteris

Yesterday we were in Freiburg – totally different from Berlin. This time Mr F and I (along with a number of regional bank dignitaries) were received by some of the city's VIPs such as the mayor and the Stellvertretender Bürgermeister, along with the regulation wives with their usual and huge lipstick smudges. There was a great deal of "*Vielen Dank für Ihren Besuch auf unserer schönen Stadt*" ("Thank you for visiting our wonderful city") repeated all day.

When we arrived at the university, beautiful and splendid, old buildings, breath of fresh air and an opportunity for me to write a little poetry, we were met by more important folk – professors and *herr* doctor professors galore. Then more cake ("*Bitte, ich fordere Sie auf ein Stück Kuchen zu nehmen. Bitte tun. Meine Frau machte es.*"), which was impossible to refuse for fear of insulting someone's wife. It's not that the cake was bad (in fact the very reverse was the case), but that there was just so much to get through.

Finally we came to the introduction of Mr F and we were off. I had made sure that technically all was correct and, this being Germany, it was. The sound, the lighting, the ambience – all good even if the auditorium was sweltering hot. Mr F fluctuated between English and German and his speech was well received. I was patted on the back and then we went for beer *und* sausage.

Arthur

>

From: Steven Charteris [stevencharteris@staracademy.com]
Sent: 07/12/2012 11.16 AM GMT
To: Arthur Shilling [arthur.shilling@gammondhopes.com]
Subject: "… we wound our modesty and make
foul the clearness of our deservings, when of
ourselves we publish them."

Arthur (or Artur, if you really must insist on the German form)

Mrs C sends her very best and it was she who suggested the line from Shakespeare above. She was, you may recall, a passable Helena in her day and knows most lines from *All's Well That Ends Well*. The Steward, who speaks this line (in Act I, scene iii) made an impression on the younger Mrs C – almost to the point where a domestic accident nearly occurred. The divorce courts beckoned for a short while.

Don't be too downhearted about the Scottish play. I'm sure that you were first class and, again, I can only apologise for not being able to witness your success. It matters not that the whole performance wasn't necessarily up to RSC standards. Well, it does matter to the extent that the audience would normally like to enjoy what's going on onstage of course. I do recall a terribly amusing production of the play in London when a very famous actor took the title role. A number of nuns walked out at half time and there was much tittering in the Upper Circle when it seemed that our hero was hanging with some desperation onto the edge of a table at the end of Act Two.

One thing. Can you please desist from what I am certain are helpful hints as to various 'treatments' in which you see fit to suggest that Mrs C should partake? Her 'situation' is under control thank you and it really is unbecoming and somewhat impertinent of someone of your years and experience to recommend Rumanian health programmes.

Now then… to business.

Modesty
- Take the Steward's and Mrs C's advice – practice modesty. You're doing well but don't let it all go to your head. Corporate life isn't always easy and you're clearly destined for good things. Mr Bose sounds to me like a good role model. Also, the good will balance the less-than-good. You'll see.

Role-play training
- Role-playing allows a group of employees to act out work scenarios. It opens communications and it puts a participant on the spot; it also helps build confidence and allows people to try out interpersonal skills ideas in some safety. Well, that's the idea certainly. Mrs C and I sometimes undertake role-play in order to manage local and household difficulties, but that's really none of your business.

- Through the use of role-play, individuals can become equipped with valuable insights and confidence in communication. Or at least that's the theory and, as you discovered, this needs preparation and very good management. I tend to agree that, in springing the exercise on you, Mr Almoun did himself no favours. Many employees, in similar situations, would not have turned up and it's quite reasonable to expect some decent notice and even time for some preparation.

- Role-play highlights the difference between how people *think* they are communicating and how their communication is *perceived* by others around them. The process encourages critical thinking such as analysis and problem-solving skills. Actors mincing about in black tights doesn't necessarily create the right atmosphere or environment. Your session should, I think, have involved professional trainers (despite Mr Almoun's undoubted zeal and enthusiasm for the actors) who should then have observed and noted in detail your behaviour and performance and that of your colleagues. Professional feedback is essential. Many trainers choose to video the role-plays and watch them again with the delegates – often on a one-to-one or small group basis.

- While this might be something that you may not care to suggest to Mr Almoun, role-playing can be used as an assessment of where someone is in terms of skills development. Many major high street store chains throughout the world use it to improve customer handling.

- The process can also be used to help people understand others – and the position of others. For example, a person can role-play a stance, argument or approach with which they disagree, to better understand that particular angle and address any areas that should be rectified.

- Training can unintentionally surface anxieties, memories, phobias – and can also trigger other emotional reactions in a small number of participants. Jonny Applebaum (aged 43), a new addition to our literature teaching staff, screamed for his mother to take away the giraffe when we undertook an exercise where inner fears were encouraged to come to the surface. Never again.

TV programmes

- I can't really comment on your raw experiences with television. The main thing is to be honest about what you *don't* know and to seek advice immediately once you encounter a problem. It was a stroke of luck (and perhaps Mr Bose's efforts) that the PR position concerning the programmes was reversed.

- I'm pleased for you that all's well that ends well, although I can't quite see why your bank is seen in a good light in its support of a violent and blossoming narcotics trade.

Handling the media

- While you didn't have a great deal to do with the media concerning the TV programmes, it might have all heated up, so it is worth knowing what to do – although I'm sure that your delightful Chloe would have come to the rescue. Or not. Give up any notions of trying to control the media. You can only control your *response* to the media.

- Establish a consistent point of contact from whom reporters can get information and press updates. This designated person should be able to respond to press inquiries and logistical questions. It certainly shouldn't be you.

- Handouts or emails with background information or answers to Frequently Asked Questions should be available. This is an opportunity to get the bank's story out there.

- Don't ever lie, mislead or talk deliberate nonsense: it will come back and hurt/haunt you or the bank every time. Don't speculate; stick to the known facts.

- Be direct and responsive. "No comment" is not a response. It gives the impression that you're trying to hide something. It's best to address questions, give whatever information you can and indicate a willingness to be helpful.

- Take the initiative – in a crisis or controversy, people are looking for leadership. State what action is being taken in response to the problem. Stay away from comments about blame, responsibility or causes until *all* the facts are available.

- Stay on track and don't let questions, reporters or even colleagues lead you astray. Awkward questions don't always require answers – they can be used to reiterate your prime message. It's fine to say, "I don't know", then commit to getting the information back to the reporter as soon as possible.

- Get rid of any jargon. Translate complicated ideas, issues or technology into plain language. Put your important points first; don't bury the main proposition. Get to the main nub of the matter as soon as possible.

- Important – you made a mistake and should have admitted that you didn't understand what Sir Christopher meant when he mentioned editing rights. Don't make that error of judgement again – admit you don't know something or ask what it means.

Germany

- It sounds as if you had a good time in *der Haupt-und Nebenstraßen in Deutschland* ('in the highways and byways of Germany' in case your language has slipped since your return). I too studied some German and know the Black Forest area a little. Mrs C and I went there some years ago – not Freiburg, but Lake Titisee. The lake is tranquil and you can take a small boat out for a picnic which indeed we did, although Mrs C did keep remarking that we had to be careful of the crocodiles. We stayed at a small inn with a widow who took great pride in her cooking and her cake I do recall was often alcohol-filled and rich. And the mushroom soup had sherry in it. It was the end of the beginning for Mrs C.

- Doing business abroad exposes people to different cultures and behaviours. Before travelling to another country, many executives tend not to consider factors such as differences in meeting etiquette, negotiation styles and business protocol. However, it is precisely these areas one should be addressing since a lack of cross-cultural understanding leads people to form stereotypes.

- Germans value their privacy. Generally and mentally there is a divide between public and private life. As a result, they wear a protective shell when doing business. This may be interpreted as coldness. However, this is not the case. After a period of time, barriers eventually fall.

- When doing business in Germany, remember that punctuality is a serious issue. Business people work hard and are under a lot of pressure. Germans typically plan

their time very carefully. It is considered bad etiquette
to be late (or indeed very early) as it shows disrespect for
people's time. Prof Meinhoffer-Bausch is often two hours
early for anything and invariably will have eaten most of
the olives at a Humanities Faculty drinks party. It has
been known that he will arrive four hours before his
flight from any airport which is little fun if you are his
travelling companion.

- In German business, meetings tend to be functional,
  formal and usually stick to a set agenda including start
  and finish times.

- Decisions are made methodically. Do not try to rush
  proceedings or apply pressure. If anything, enquire about
  areas in which you may be able to provide additional or
  more specific information. Try and back up information
  with insight from personal experience. Once a decision has
  been reached, minds are very rarely changed.

- I've dined with you on a few occasions Arthur and can verify
  that your table manners are impeccable apart from your
  habit of eating melon as if you're on a desert island.

- Cultural clashes are not limited to individuals or groups
  discussing or negotiating a business deal. An entire company
  can suffer from cultural differences. The $36 billion
  acquisition of Chrysler by Germany's Daimler-Benz in
  1998 was marked by a most significant cultural clash in
  the business world. The aim of the merger was to create an
  international automotive superbrand, but it didn't happen.
  When DaimlerChrysler sold the Chrysler group, the latter

reported a $2 billion first-quarter loss. Culture clash alone doesn't fully explain the failure of the venture, but it was a destructive element apparent from the start. After the merger, German and American executives apparently spent a lot of time deciding on the size of the new company's business card. Would it follow the small American-size card or the larger size common in Europe? That sort of nonsense multiplied by a million similar wrangles will always destroy the greater good.

Well now, I can hear Mrs C calling, so I had better run. I also have to mark a number of essays on the topic: 'Mercutio is considered to be one of Shakespeare's great creations, yet he is killed relatively early in the play. What therefore makes Mercutio so memorable a character?' Forgive the split infinitive.

Anyway, good luck with Aguecheek. Mrs C and I will definitely come down and see that. It'll be fun and perhaps we can have dinner afterwards, although Mrs C has to be in bed by 10PM.

By the way, you mention that Mr Staffordshire uses capital letters in the content of his emails. You, and indeed he, should know that it's considered very bad manners to do that and is the equivalent of shouting. Mind you, I'd advise not telling him this – although you could mention it to Mr Bose.

Take care, Arthur. I really can't manage Artur. It sounds like a small part character from a loose Austrian opera of small renown.

Regards

Steven Charteris

Chapter EIGHT

"Shall I compare thee to a summer's day?
Thou art more lovely and more temperate:
Rough winds do shake the darling buds of May,
And summer's lease hath all too short a date."

From Shakespeare's *Sonnet 18*

71

From: Arthur Shilling [arthur.shilling@gammondhopes.com]
Sent: 07/14/2012 06.16 AM GMT
To: Steven Charteris [stevencharteris@staracademy.com]
Subject: "When sorrows come, they come not single spies, but in battalions."

Steven

Someone left me a handwritten note with the above quotation – 'When the sorrows come…' and nothing more, although the note did say Act IV, scene iv when everyone knows it's scene v which means either this someone doesn't know their *Hamlet* or the mistake was deliberate. But why? What? How?

Anyway, I suppose the quote could be worse. I have my suspicions about the culprit. It could be Jenny Barstiff because she enjoys bad news (for others) and she seems to delight in my woes often by dancing the Twist or giving me a flavour of *Madame Butterfly*, although I suspect that Giacomo Puccini would have had heart palpitations if he could have been here in Canary Wharf last Tuesday at 2PM. Another culprit might be Mrs Sourdough who also lives in the world of high drama and has just begun an evening class in 'Shakespeare and the Modern Kitchen'. I'm sure that the message was well meant.

I came slightly unstuck a few days ago – or rather, I didn't. Over the weekend my delectable landlady, the lovely Victoria Holyhead, had just returned from a job in Malta making up some people to look like prison inmates who'd been forgotten for twenty years. She was slightly ratty because she'd had little sleep and some hair glue had leaked all over her clothes in her suitcase. She said that she'd like to practice putting a gash on my face. This being Sunday evening and with nothing else to do – and with the opportunity to be inches from the red-haired temptress, I readily agreed. Half an hour later I had a gash on my left cheek and a smashing dog bite on my right. I looked really good. Or bad, depending on your point of view. Then she looked askance and shrieked, "Oh no, I left the silicon glue remover in Malta! Sorry Arthur but you're stuck with the wounds until tomorrow evening!"

I wept and gnashed my teeth and even tried prising off the latex wounds from my face, but that only succeeded in ripping my real skin so I stopped that course of action. Plus I had a meeting the next day that I couldn't avoid. So, I had to construct a story and fast. Mrs Sourdough was the first to react. "Told you so," she shouted with some unnecessary glee. "The runes were right. You got my 'battalions' message? I didn't understand it properly of course but it was quoted in my paper and your stars are the same as mine." Without any concern for my face, she trotted off. Then Mr Almoun bounced up and said, "Wow! Wonder what the other guy must look like. Well done you bro." He punched me on the shoulder and ran off, weaving in and out of spaces between people minding their own business in the corridor. Then it was Jez Staffordshire who espied me and said something like, "Shouldn't you be in hospital or hat the werry least have hay bandage on dat?" Then, woe is me, I had the worst lift ride ever. Everyone in the lift just stared goggled-eyed at my wounds. Those nearest winced and many missed their floors because they were so entranced. I just smiled and that must have looked weird. It was very hot in the lift.

I spent the day with my hands on my face which must have looked very odd, not least in my meeting which was attended briefly by Sir Christopher. He did a double-take and then stared. "Dear me, dear me," was all he grated and then left shaking his head. Only Mr Bose smiled.

Luckily, when I got home, my red-haired minx had the ready mixture with which to remove said wounds. I refused to say anything and I'm sure that guilt is in the air, although her giggling seemed to indicate that this wasn't the case. The next day was funny because people thought that I'd had some miraculous recovery, particularly Mrs Sourdough who is wont to be of a religious nature when it so suits.

Best

Arthur

72

From: Arthur Shilling [arthur.shilling@gammondhopes.com]
Sent: 07/17/2012 05.16 AM GMT
To: Steven Charteris [stevencharteris@staracademy.com]
Subject: Language

Dear Steven

English has been a problem recently. Mr F has said that we need to become more adept at good English – in speeches, in emails, in reports and so on. In a beautifully-written email to the department, he maintained that our punctuation, spelling and sentence construction was appalling and needed addressing immediately. He would, he maintained, establish some classes for those who sought assistance or who would benefit most.

I must presume that the email does not refer to the likes of me. Mrs Sourdough could benefit from some tuition and so too could Mr Almoun, although please don't ever tell him that I said so!

At a departmental meeting with Mr F, he abandoned the agenda and described some English language conundrums. He said (and I quote verbatim because I wrote the whole thing down) that we had a box and the plural is boxes but we have an ox and the plural is oxen not oxes. We have a goose (at Christmas in Germany he said) and two of that bird are called geese. However, he said, there is the animal called a moose but the plural is not meese. There is one mouse (and here Mrs Sourdough looked at the floor nervously) but many are called mice. But, went on Mr F, the plural of house is houses not hice. The plural of man is men but the plural of pan isn't pen. The plural of foot is feet, but the plural of boot isn't beet. One tooth is a tooth, but a whole set are teeth. Then (and even Mr F was sweating a bit at this point) the plural of booth should be beeth. The plural of that is those but the plural of hat isn't hose and the plural of cat is cats not cose. The masculine pronouns are he, his and him (and by now Mr F was looking worried and beginning to lose the plot) but the feminine isn't she, shis and shim. "*Genug ist genug vorläufig,*" ("Enough is enough for the time being") Mr F muttered, and stirred his peppermint tea with some vigour.

At another meeting, Jez Staffordshire said that he'd had a number of complaints from 'hupstairs' (and here he glanced upwards at the ceiling in case we weren't sure where 'hupstairs' was). He said that apparently our telephone manner was poor and that our tone of voice was not worthy of a department with the word 'communications' in the title. This, went on Jez, jowls awobbling, would have to stop and we'd all need to get a grip. He wanted to get an external firm to come in and train us in telephone techniques. Mrs Sourdough, who had once managed a call centre in Edinburgh, said that she thought this was a very good idea and everyone else groaned. As if I don't have enough to do what with role-playing evenings, language training and my rehearsals for *Twelfth Night*!

Much grumbling around the water coolers I can tell you.

Best

Arthur

73

From: Arthur Shilling [arthur.shilling@gammondhopes.com]
Sent: 07/22/2012 04.16 AM GMT
To: Steven Charteris [stevencharteris@staracademy.com]
Subject: Off to foreign climes once more!

Steven

Ha! Am off to Dubai (again!) for the Chairman's Strategic Forum which, as I mentioned, is now on its second tour of duty. Derek Rattles has been with the Chairman for much of the tour but he, Mr R, has to have what he calls "a small procedure" that will keep him in hospital for a few days with more to recuperate. Deaf Knee has asked for me by name to be part of the team! There you are. Success and recognition! We're off in a few days which is great, because I'll miss a whole chunk of the extra-mural classes. Phooey to language and telephony classes. I have to say, though, that our director for *Twelfth Night*, the fragrant Linda Nookles, is less than pleased because we're at a stage when 'books should be down' i.e. lines should be learnt and in our heads. They are not in mine yet. She says that I can't rehearse the famous and comedic fight scene with a book in my hand. I have practised my lines at home although Victoria Holyhead told me to a) shut up and b) shut up – doubly so because she was trying to watch *X Factor* and didn't I have anything better to do than to burble Shakespeare, make horrendous 'have at ye' noises and thump around from settee to chair and back to settee again?

Preparation for one of the Chairman's Forums is fairly straightforward now. You'll recall that the events are designed to present a view of the world in 2030 for the bank's top cadre. Dubai is to be quite a big show with 900 people in two sittings.

I am very excited, although Mr Bose told me to calm down and Jenny Barstiff had another go at the *Dance of the Seven Veils* as she shimmied by.

Arthur

74

From: Arthur Shilling [arthur.shilling@gammondhopes.com]
Sent: 07/27/2012 03.16 AM GMT
To: Steven Charteris [stevencharteris@staracademy.com]
Subject: American intern

Stevie baby

Howya doin'? We have an American intern who's been shipped in for two months from our New York office. She's very pretty and her name is Al. When I asked if this was short for anything, she just stared and asked if Arthur was short for something. I have to spend a little time with Al to explain how my part of the department works. She responded to every sentence I uttered with a "Yeah?" or "Cool." or "That's soooo real." or "Like, wow, for sure?" The gentle uplift at the end of her sentences became very irritating so I cut short our session with a hard look at my watch. I handed young Al over to Mrs Sourdough who was really annoyed that she had to stop her online booking for a holiday in Edinburgh with her sister: "We never miss the festival you know. You don't know what new culture, or some such thing, is around the corner, do you?"

We've just been told that the Chairman's Forum after Dubai will be here in London and that the whole department is invited to attend. Dephne wants me to be involved in that event too so my cup runneth over at the moment. Also, Mr F thinks that that we should film the London version and that the Chairman should have makeup so I've asked my delicious landlady if she'd oblige. Mr F was impressed at the speed of my response. I think he remembers my red-haired wunderkind from the last time she was in and I suspect that he took a shine to her then as did everyone else. Apart from Gordon!

Must rush because there's an emergency telephony management meeting and we have to explain why our telephone manner hasn't improved. Mine's impeccable of course, although Al, our intern, says "Hiya, Al Marshland-Hills here, how c'n I he'p you?" She then proceeds not listen to a word the caller is saying, ending with "Sorry, bud but I caint he'p yo'. Bye now. You hev yoursel' a nice day." I was horrified to find gum stuck under my desk!

I have to go and meet our esteemed Chairman with Mr Bose, Deaf Knee and an assortment of writers and PAs.

Best (or 'lader' as Al would have it)

Arthur

75

From: Arthur Shilling [arthur.shilling@gammondhopes.com]
Sent: 08/02/2012 02.16 AM GMT
To: Steven Charteris [stevencharteris@staracademy.com]
Subject: Performances

Steven

Couldn't sleep so I thought I'd bother you.

Al got shipped back to the US of A and Mrs Sourdough was dismayed because they both shared a liking for horoscopes and astrology. Everyone else was mightily relieved y'all.

The rehearsals for TN are going reasonably well although the chap playing Sir Toby Belch has terrible body odour and anyone close to him on stage has trouble focussing upon lines and moves – my good self included. Sir Toby is blissfully unaware of the problem and, in attempting to practice what he calls 'good acting', keeps leaning in for his asides and drunken phrases. The recipient of the terrible breath and poor underarm freshness leans as far back as physiology will allow, causing huge mirth to those watching. Our director has yelled more than once that this "will not do", but she has refused thus far to have words where words are required.

Other than this problem, my fight scenes are coming on apace and we have a fight arranger chap from RADA who is ever patient in showing us what's what, although when our lisping colleague (this time playing Malvolio) tries to escape the dungeon and attempts to fight one and all, the fight instructor clutches his head with what we can only think is an onset of migraine.

The remedial English classes are at lunchtimes every Tuesday and initially everyone attended, but now it's just two or three. Mr F had a fit when he realised that people weren't taking the matter seriously, so Messrs Bose, Rattles, Almoun and Staffordshire were called in for a huge telling off apparently and now we all have to be at the wretched classes where we 'learn' punctuation, phraseology and vocabulary. Mr McMonkey (I think that's his name), from Glasgow University, contributes to our education with strange guttural comments, the majority of which nobody can understand. To cover up my incomprehension, when asked a question I always pretend to be having a coughing fit, but on one occasion he proceeded to give me the Heimlich Manoeuvre.

I've been spending considerable time preparing the content and organising the contributors for the Dubai Forum. The production company is a new one and the producer, content specialists, production manager and other assorted fellows are being very helpful and polite. Jenny is kindly helping to arrange the speakers/ contributors and, while we're using some of those who've helped us before, there's a need for some new blood – besides which, some of the fees being asked by the 'old guard' are horrendous. Jez is controversial in his recommendation of speakers and tries to go as left wing as he can possibly manage. Consequently, he was beginning to select a team of what I can only call Trotskyites and communists ranging from dark pink to bright red. Deaf Knee was insane with anger and summoned Jez (and self) to her office. Jez enquired after her health and then I'm surprised that his hair remained on his head such was the vent of spleen and breath from my diminutive colleague. If Jez was confident when he came into Dephne's office, he had somewhat stooped shoulders as he left. Such is show business.

Off for a drink later with the fabulous Chloe!

Best

Arthur

76

From: Arthur Shilling [arthur.shilling@gammondhopes.com]
Sent: 08/06/2012 23.16 PM GMT
To: Steven Charteris [stevencharteris@staracademy.com]
Subject: Birthday!

Steven

It's my birthday! Yey! Many thanks indeed for your kind card. Please also pass on my thanks to Mrs C who will undoubtedly have spent an age making the card. She must have used a vast amount of rice and pasta, but the effect is remarkable. I hope that the red blobs are paint. They are, aren't they?

The office was very kind and I had good wishes from everyone including a formal email from HR which was addressed Dear Mr Shillingses and complemented me on my 44th birthday! What the hey? Mr Bose gave me a musical card that played a version of Happy Birthday in a Dixieland sort of style, Jenny B gave me a small cake that she'd made herself and Mrs Sourdough gave me some vouchers for a pizza outlet. The drama mob gave me four bottles of assorted beers (leftovers from a party I think – but it's the thought that counts) and last night we went to the Canary Wharf Curry Parlour and they bought me dinner which was very kind. I filled up on poppadoms which is always an error of judgement. My landlady, the effervescent Victoria Holyhead, has promised to cook me a Cordon Bleu dinner – interesting since I've only ever seen her make Jamie Oliver 30-minute meals which tend to take her somewhat longer.

At the last lunchtime English language class, we addressed spelling and common difficulties or mistakes. I had a small snooze. The Scottish gentleman is no more and the newbie is a woman from a commercial operation that offers these sorts of courses. Only problem is she begins each sentence with "Aaaarm" which, after a while, is infuriating. But she's nice enough and went through things like the common confusion between 'lose' and 'loose', 'its' and 'it's', 'their' and 'there', 'effect' and 'affect', 'your' and 'you're'. And then we had a whole host of common spelling errors: again 'they're', 'their', 'there', 'definitely' and 'definately', 'whether' and 'weather' and… oh for goodness' sake!

I am swimming in plain English, crunching my teeth at Mrs Sourdough's misunderstanding of the fact that parrot has two 'r's and offering a mental toast to Richard Hoggart's classic *The Uses of Literacy* (1957), a tome that was introduced to the Shilling reading list by your good self.

Arthur

77

From: Arthur Shilling [arthur.shilling@gammondhopes.com]
Sent: 08/12/2012 11.16 PM GMT
To: Steven Charteris [stevencharteris@staracademy.com]
Subject: The Orient beckons again and fable will become fact

Steven

I've been reading up on the Orient – gleam of vaunted gold, the gems of Samarkand, the vast sands, the maps of secret treasure, the mysterious Cathay, the enchantment that is Persia, the pleasures of Araby, the warriors of Abyssinia, the veils of the harem, the walls of sunlit and jasmine-scented gardens where nightingales eternally warble to the rose, the secretive women of ruby lips (but not smudged lipstick), the pale pearls and ringlets like, um, hyacinths. An oriental Juliet gazes from her high window and watches over lithe ladies who weave their dancing way through innumerable courtyards, adorned with diamonds nourished by the dew of heaven. And always the pomegranates are melting with sweetness.

Hey, what do you think? Good stuff huh? I am destined for a world where true love and salvation return with warriors long thought dead, doom and tragedy ever at their heels. I follow in the footsteps of Byron, Shelley and Tennyson all of whom drew on the same charming, exotic, escapist myth. I am told by Mrs Sourdough that I should prepare for malaria.

Anyway, reality hit with something of a bump because Mr Flattergleich has asked me to take the remaining English language classes before I journey East. Apparently the lady with the "Aaaaahm" problem has been fired. Pah! As if I haven't got better things to do. Mind you, the PR department's been forced to attend as well, so at least I shall have dear Chloe upon whose visage I can gaze while the doves flutter. Perhaps I'm getting a tad carried away with the idea of Eastern promise and ladies of the night. Not that Chloe is a lady of the night. At least, I don't believe that she is.

Also, Mr F's tasked me with writing two speeches before I depart – one on the growing need for continued education in business and the other on third world debt and new ways of managing the same.

Aye me, too much, too much. But, what through yonder window breaks? Toby Belch that's what. Our *Twelfth Night* director, Ms Linda Nookles, plucked up courage and throwing caution to the wind, talked to our very smelly Sir Toby Belch. In horror and some embarrassment, he stepped backwards and fell through the set's window which of course was made of thin plastic. We heard the sobbing for ages afterwards. He locked himself in the ladies' toilets (the gents' not functioning that evening) much to the dismay of all the cast, particularly the ladies. Eventually he emerged, head low, and with a sad shuffle trudged off to the Underground. We all felt very guilty but, I have to say, relieved.

Much concern about the speakers for Dubai. Professor Duncan Waspblain, due to speak on the technology of the future, had something of an accident when cleaning his teeth apparently. No, I don't know either. And Shoshana Shavit, a retired senior officer from Mossad, has been recalled for duty and has to return to Israel immediately. That's not all – Roberta Tululi Eyeai, the well known Sunday paper editor, has declined to take part at the eleventh hour because her husband has left her for another man. All hands to the pumps – well mine certainly – to find good replacements. Jenny was offered as a helpmate by Mr Rattles (Jez having the sulks) but she wasn't much help and the production agency was really of little aid either. The agency has got on our collective nerves recently (billing, promises not kept, never the same team, intelligence not widely shared – in all senses).

My concubines salute you (if only).

Arthur of Arabia

78

From: Arthur Shilling [arthur.shilling@gammondhopes.com]
Sent: 08/15/2012 06.16 AM GMT
To: Steven Charteris [stevencharteris@staracademy.com]
Subject: Dubai, Dubai, so good they named it twice (although of course they didn't)

Dear Steven

Am in Dubai once more! The event's all set. We found replacements for everyone and, some say, better than the originals. Please thank Mrs C for her email containing some outstanding suggestions, although we couldn't really use the Chief Rabbi or that gentleman from Turkmenstan or indeed the Chief of Staff from North Korea. How does she *know* such folk?

Dubai eh? It's amazing. Our hotel is brilliant (in all senses – lots of gold leaf abounds). I did get a shock on arrival as I did the first time because everything is indeed so bright, new and different, yet very Western. On the plane (business class!) I sat next to a very interesting fellow who was in the clothing trade and he gave me a lecture about UAE dress. The majority of men wear a long-sleeved, one-piece thing called a *dishdashah, thoub* or *kandura* that covers the whole body. This garment allows the air to circulate, which helps cool the body during the hot summer days. I will definitely get one. During summer, the *dishdashah* is usually made of white cotton to reflect sunlight. In winter, it's made from heavier fabric such as wool and comes in darker colours. Perhaps, asked my aircraft chum, I'd like to see some examples? But there was a movie I wanted to see and so I declined firmly. He was not deterred and went on to explain more. The *guthra* is the headscarf sported by men. The most popular colours are plain white, or red and white checks. These checks are traditional to the Bedouin. Nowadays, you can get any colour. Was there a colour that I liked best? No there bloody well wasn't was what I wanted to say, but of course didn't.

He went on. The *egal* is the black rope that fixes the headscarf in place. In days gone by, these would be used by Bedouin to tie their camel's feet down during the night while they were travelling. I wonder, Steven, if I have some Bedouin blood in me. Worth exploring. More of the younger nationals these days do not wear their *egal* and tie their *guthra* in a different way on their head. This is called *hamdaniya*. Look closely at a man's *kandura* ("Forgive the impertinence," my fellow traveller quipped) and you will see a small string-like contraption flowing from the neck. This is the *kerkusha*. Some liken it to a tie and it is not always worn, though those who do wear the *kerkusha* are sometimes inclined to play around with it. Those in power can be seen wearing the *bisht* (which is similar to a jacket) that is worn on top of the *kandura*. The *bisht* is also donned for special occasions such as *Eid* or weddings, for example, and also when visiting a Sheikh. A *faneela* is a vest worn under the *kandura* and a *woozar* is a piece of white cloth which is tied around the waist under the *kandura*. I did stifle a yawn at this stage but the gent took no notice. He explained that *na-aal* are the sandals worn by men and at this point he waved his feet around showing proudly that he was sporting a pair.

My aircraft buddy went on to explain that I should stick to the laws of the land and then I should be fine. "Walking around in hot pants and a tank top simply won't work in the UAE and no kissing on the beach," he said, and I was slightly boggle-eyed that he thought I should do such a thing.

Luckily lunch was then served and he finished with, "As a rule of thumb for females, they should dress Western in Dubai, a little more conservative in Abu Dhabi and they must cover their skin in Sharjah, except for their face, neck and hands. Or else." And then he ate his lunch and went to sleep. I watched my film but as the titles rolled I did wonder if I could change my name to Orrance. Maybe not. Have you seen *Lawrence of Arabia*? Brilliant.

The Chairman's Forum will take place in our hotel's auditorium, which is well-equipped, albeit a tad gaudy for my tastes. It's just wonderful to consider that I'm in the Arabian Peninsular. The man in the lift gave me his card and said that he was in charge of the city's tourism. He said, "Dubai's dynamics are always transient and ever-changing with its constant urge to construct something better and bigger than the previous." "Oh yes? The previous what?" I asked. "What do you mean 'previous what?'" the man said in some confusion, relieved to find that the lift had reached the 20th floor which was his stop. Or at least he said it was.

We have been afforded every courtesy and the production company has behaved impeccably, apart from one very unfortunate incident when I stepped backwards to look at the set and promptly trod on Raspberry Jenkins' iPad which apparently she'd only bought that day! The crew laughed and laughed. What the iPad was doing on the floor I don't know but Rasp was incandescent.

Another unfortunate incident occurred. We are having some interactive percussion for the mid-session of the event to engage the audience. I'd seen it done elsewhere and was convinced that a drumming workshop would unite our delegates through rhythm! With a drum for each participant, the group would be led on an exhilarating rhythmic adventure. Within minutes, I was convinced, energy levels would be heightened. The drummers are a part of a local troupe based in Dubai. The lead drummer had a wild look and was dressed in jeans and scruffy t-shirt with 'Bad Moon Rising' on the front. He was more than mildly upset when I asked him his business. "What does it look like? I'm carrying a drum." Well a) I considered that rude and b) he clearly didn't realise that I was his client. "It's OK Jack," yelled Raspberry looking meanly in my direction, "He's just the client and he breaks things. Watch out for your drum."

Unfortunately for her, she didn't see Dephne Hong standing two metres behind her. Both Rasp and this Jack person were quick-marched out of the auditorium and all we heard was a loud, "Do. You. Understand?" and "Do. You. Want. More. Work. From. Us?" and a few mumbled arrangements of "Yes" and "Yeah". I danced a small jig. The end result was that Raspberry came over to apologise to me and the drum leader also said something like "Sorry mate. No 'ard feelin's – nah wod ah mean?"

I must run now because many of our speakers have arrived and rehearsals will begin shortly. That of course means eons of PowerPoint and I dread the hours ahead!

كبيرة متعة الأسرة أن لكم هل ,اليوم رائعا يكون وقد

(Have a wonderful day and may you and your family have great joy.)

The Bedouin and I are as one

Arthur of the Desert

79

From: Arthur Shilling [arthur.shilling@gammondhopes.com]
Sent: 08/16/2012 13.16 PM GMT
To: Steven Charteris [stevencharteris@staracademy.com]
Subject: Dubai encore

Steven

One of our contributors had trouble getting into the country, but we don't know why. Another cried off at the last minute which made Dephne throw her mobile phone into the sea, something she instantly regretted. But all was fine really. Our Chairman acquitted himself very well and indeed, afterwards, complimented both Dephne and the bank's team (including me), although Raspberry Jenkins, hopping from foot to foot at the circle's edge, was ignored.

Jack and his drummers did a good job and were well received. This evening there's dinner in the dessert amongst the Bedouin, although frankly I think that there won't be any real Bedouin. I must check up on the Shilling family tree.

Tomorrow I shall have a day of R&R if Deaf Knee allows it. I've been invited for tea at the Burj Al-Arab with some regional bank dignitaries, although one did whisper to me in the style of a verbal brochure that "Everyone dreams of staying at the Burj Al-Arab, the most extravagant hotel in the world. However, Mr Shilling, the world's first seven star hotel chooses its customers and not vice versa. Burj Al Arab's billowing sail enjoys being a focus of public attention with its glittery gold interiors, ultra-spacious suites and the heightened level of luxury offered. See you tomorrow, *Inshallah*." This evening we must get underway early because the sight of the sunset over the desert is something I'm told that my customers and I should not miss. So, 400 folk in 4x4s and off we go!

Arthur, he of a thousand cuts and fifteen wives

80

From: Arthur Shilling [arthur.shilling@gammondhopes.com]
Sent: 08/17/2012 23.16 PM GMT
To: Steven Charteris [stevencharteris@staracademy.com]
Subject: Arthur, prince of the desert

Dear Steven

Well, the desert was wonderful. At least the sunset was. I stood on a hillock gazing over the darkening sands and just gaped in wonder at the utter beauty. Then the stars – bright white and shooting on occasion. Just amazing. And the moon – nearly full and huge in the deep blue-black sky.

The dinner was less of a success. Nobody could really see what they were eating and lying on cushions isn't that easy a position when trying to eat. The Romans must have done something clever with their lying down, lounging and eating. Also the belly dancers, not, I confess, the youngest I would have chosen, were slightly oiled and some of our delegates became over-excited. But, by and large, everyone seemed to enjoy the evening and we didn't lose anyone, although Mr Almoun did go missing for an hour. Land of his fathers maybe?

When we got back to the city it was late, but some of the delegates went off to the Kasbar, a local nightclub. I went for a short while to ensure that all was well but, having a headache, couldn't really muster enthusiasm for the exotic ambiance, the mix of Arabic and western tunes, bar games, live music, the DJ and a seemingly vibrating dance floor.

The Chairman, who didn't attend the evening's 'do', was still up and about when I got back to the hotel. He and some senior execs were at the bar in shirtsleeves no less and having an animated discussion about something. I was nodded at as I went past. I said "good evening" and went to my room only to find that I'd lost my key card in the desert and had to wearily tromp back down fifty floors to the reception area where a big argument ensued, during which I lost my temper and caused people arriving at the hotel – including the Chairman's party – to turn and stare.

I really must check out my Bedouin status. We met some in the desert and a few were tall with blue eyes. Some wore smoky blue headscarves and I asked if I might buy one. When I got back to my room (eventually) a blue headscarf was on my desk, beautifully wrapped and boxed. I tried it on (scarf, not box) and marvelled at my Arabian look. I shall wear it when I go on the balloon flight tomorrow but perhaps not when I see my senior colleagues at the Burj Al Arab Hotel.

To sleep now. My goats are tethered and my palaces are clean. My gold glitters. My rubies sparkle or rather my diamonds do. My rubies just wink. My followers wrap themselves against the desert cold. The moon shines brightly in its sickle form. And all of Arabia rests. But Arthur has one eye open.

>

From: Steven Charteris [stevencharteris@staracademy.com]
Sent: 08/20/2012 11.16 AM GMT
To: Arthur Shilling [arthur.shilling@gammondhopes.com]
Subject: "Do not do too much with your own hands"

Arthur

You are not related to any Bedouin.

The subject quote is from T. E. Lawrence and taken from a guide he wrote for British officers in the *Arab Bulletin* (20 August 1917). I mention it only because you are clearly taking on a great deal now and you must be very honest with your managers when you cannot acquit everything as well as you might. By the way, you could do worse than read Lawrence's *Seven Pillars of Wisdom* – it's very good.

Effective communication

- Good quality communication is essential to the success of any business. Many businesses create problems for themselves with poor internal communication. So, Mr F and co are right to be concerned if they feel that telephony and quality of writing are poor.

- When customers or colleagues call a business or a department, they hope to get someone on the line who is helpful, friendly and positive. When you answer the phone, your tone of voice communicates a message in the first few seconds. Your tone of voice could let the other party know that you are excited about the opportunity to serve and solve problems. But you may instead communicate that the other party is a bother and a waste of your time. Smile before answering the phone and the customer will hear that smile in your voice.

- If you don't listen fully to each message left by a colleague or customer, you will likely miss a key piece of information.

- Interrupting someone is rude and it also shows your lack of willingness to help. Listen with an open mind and a willingness to change your viewpoint if you are wrong. I cannot begin to understand how your American intern lasted five minutes in the States, never mind here! Lazy telephone technique is inexcusable.

- Give people on the phone a reason to trust you and keep that trust by sticking to your word and fulfilling your promises.

- In business (and actually in academia too), finding the cause of recurring problems is important. Sometimes, however, the fault-finding becomes personal and unproductive. The goal of identifying mistakes should be correcting the problem. Finding what went wrong and how to fix it is a much better use of time than finding out who is to blame.

Language

Despite your reticence, which I did find a trifle irritating, it's not such a bad idea for a business to want to improve communication amongst its staff. Why not? And, by the way, arrogance is not a good or useful trait Arthur, so please desist.

Some reminders for you to pass on as you feel relevant. Make of this what you will:

- No word in the English language rhymes with month. 'Dreamt' is the only English word that ends in the letters 'mt'. The word 'set' has more definitions than any other word in the English language.

- There are only four words in the English language which end in '-dous' – tremendous, horrendous, stupendous and hazardous. No words in the English language rhyme with orange, silver or purple (as I discovered to my cost when trying to win the Golden Verse Poetry Competition in my youth).

- Mrs C just now wondered why people recite at a play but play at a recital. From the kitchen she shouted, "I wonder why grocers don't groce and hammers don't ham." There was a moment's hiatus then came the next contribution: "Why," she squealed in some indignation, "do we have noses that run and feet that smell? Surely that's the wrong way round? And how can a slim chance and a fat chance be the same?" Then there was a silence and I knew that I had not locked away Jameson's finest. Mind you, and luckily, there was only a drop left and the results weren't too chaotic or bruising.

The art of good writing

- George Orwell, in the excellent *Politics and the English Language* (1946), declared that there are six rules of clear English. I quote:

  1. Never use a metaphor, simile or other figure of speech which you are used to seeing in print.
  2. Never use a long word when a short one will do.
  3. If it is possible to cut a word out, always cut it out.
  4. Never use the passive where you can use the active.
  5. Never use a foreign phrase, a scientific word, or a jargon word if you can think of an everyday English equivalent.
  6. Break any of these rules sooner than say anything outright barbarous.

- With the simple click of a mouse button (although 'simple' isn't strictly true since Mrs C struggles with IT and we have gone through a fair few laptops for all sorts of reasons), we can find information about all kinds of topics, companies, products and services from all over the world. The world presents an abundance of new opportunities and English is the common denominator and a prerequisite for international recognition.

- Most people in business have a good command of the English language but we must not presume. They may be proficient enough to verbally convey their companies' first-class products, leading know-how and services. Yet, that same language proficiency often becomes a stumbling block when one has to present one's corporate advantages (or anything) with equal excellence in writing. Writing in English is challenging. Great caution must be exercised because what matters is not only what you say but *how* you say it. Witness Professor Snickerblade who ordered 1,500 turtles instead of 15 books on the mythology of turtles. The case is still ongoing.

- A flawless and professionally written text is a must to boost one's chances for success whether in regular communications, in sales, in PR or in business anywhere.

- At one time or another all of us have stumbled across badly written material, spelling mistakes or grammatical errors – perfect grounds for embarrassment and misunderstandings. You remember Johnathan Pewynasty? Well, he hadn't a clue and regularly insulted the Dean with his dreadful emails and appalling essays. Mind you, I understand that Johnathan is now editor of some magazine or other in Uganda.

- Certainly, good writing takes time and a lot of energy. A skilled business writer has the right words handy to convey values, a corporate philosophy and the unique company spirit. If you are one of these, Arthur, then there is nothing wrong in helping others.

The art of good communication
- Be clear about what you are trying to achieve.

- Companies and departments should encourage a two-way flow of information between managers and direct reports. Managers should:
    - hold regular meetings (face-to-face is invariably better than sending an email),
    - use language that colleagues will understand – not jargon,

— keep discussions focused, relevant, local, brief and timely,
— use open-ended questions to draw out ideas from colleagues,
— ensure that communications reach every relevant employee, and
— use social events to break down barriers and build trust.

- Face-to-face communication is a direct and effective way to get across facts. It can't be relied upon completely because misunderstandings can arise, so written communication is a good supplement.

- Effective written communication is typically accurate, brief and clear. It's good practice to have copies of all business policies and information in one place to which employees have access, such as an intranet site.

- There are many mistakes made in written English which, with a little care, could be avoided. Here are a few of my favourites:

  — Tense refers to time. What time is it in your sentence? Whatever time it is it should remain consistent throughout your whole piece of writing. If it was last week you are talking about, stay there. There are three tenses in writing – past, present and future. Pick a tense and stick to it.

  — Spelling is one of the most important things and, without it, you can kiss your credibility goodbye. Spell-checkers are poor substitutes for knowing how to spell and can leave behind more errors than you realise. There are many different forms of words and your spell-checker won't know which form you want to use.

— A run-on sentence is one that is simply too long. Usually, a run-on sentence can be made into two or more sentences with some punctuation and style. An example of a run-on sentence might be: "Arthur and I walked over to the bar to get something to drink, but it was closed so we didn't know what to do so we kept walking until we saw a restaurant and decided to go in and get something to eat but Arthur didn't want to eat there so we kept going for another mile." Break up the sentence into smaller, more coherent parts.

— It is very important to know your punctuation, even if you never plan on using a semicolon. The most important thing to learn is where to put your commas, a common mistake among writers. Commas are used to separate parts of sentences that stand alone, such as those that are parenthetical. For example, "There were too many flowers, not that Arthur minded, but they took up most of the room." Semicolons and colons are important too – I could write reams on this topic but Mrs C is calling and I must see to her needs.

Forgive me for not being to be able to come to London to see you in *Twelfth Night*. I know I promised and I know too that you anticipated our arrival with some relish, but Mrs C really isn't up to being amongst crowds. I'm sure that you did astoundingly well I'm also sure that many will have applauded your comedic abilities. Next time, next time.

Best

Professor Charteris

Chapter Nine

"Done to death by slanderous tongue
Was the Hero that here lies…"

Claudio: *Much Ado About Nothing* (V, iii)

80

From: Arthur Shilling [arthur.shilling@gammondhopes.com]
Sent: 09/03/2012 20.16 PM GMT
To: Steven Charteris [stevencharteris@staracademy.com]
Subject: The plots thicken

Dear Steven

Well, lots to tell, dear Professor. Firstly thanks for the missive. Of course I was disappointed that you and Mrs C couldn't attend TN. It was a great success if I do say so myself. My Aguecheek was possibly better than my Bottom (which is saying something) and was certainly on par with my Mercutio. We were given a standing ovation on the first night and my delicious landlady Victoria did my makeup and produced some brilliant slashes and wounds for my appearance after the fight scene. Two ladies in the front row actually gasped in horror, so real were they. Mr Bose came round to the green room afterwards and presented me shyly with a bottle of bubbly and then was gone before I could introduce him to the cast. Mrs Sourdough hung on my neck for a moment and then hung on to Toby Belch's neck overlong.

Dubai is now a fond memory. Everyone says how well the two events went. Mr Almoun is in fine spirits and keeps saying "*Sabah el kheer*" ("Good morning") even when it isn't. Either that or he exclaims "*Kaifa haloka?*" ("How are you?"). Well that soon stopped when Mr Bose replied with "*Ana bekhair, shokran!*" ("I'm fine, thanks!")

Am already preparing for the Chairman's Strategic Forum here in London. Three showings over two days. And it's going to be filmed, although we're having some difficulty with some contributors' agents saying that they want more money for film rights.

Interesting news! There's a new position in the department – Senior Executive in charge of events. Various people have dropped hints that I should apply and so I have – rather a complex and time-consuming business. Jez Staffordshire looked at me oddly when I told him of my plans, but that could have been his usual dyspepsia. Mrs Sourdough has made encouraging noises (although those too may be diet related) and Dephne Hong has said that she'll support my application. Slight fly in the ointment – have just discovered that Raspberry Jenkins (she whose iPad I trashed) is the daughter of Mr Rattles' best friend, so she may yet scupper my chances.

Last night of *Twelfth Night* tonight! Could be a good one. Everyone's very positive. Toby Belch has washed and takes a modicum of peppermint mouthwash before he goes onstage, so all's well on that score. Really sorry that you two couldn't be here.

I've decided to discard any thoughts of Bedouin ancestry not least because, when I wore my blue headscarf to the office, security was called and it was only the intervention of Mr Alan Trebbish, our beloved Head Receptionist that saved me a visit to the local police station. Plus, everyone on my floor laughed and Mr Bose just shook his head. I've since discovered that I have some Arthurian blood and might indeed be related to King Arthur himself. It is being researched as we speak, although Jenny Barstiff says that I'm really bonkers and mental.

The Chairman's Forum London dates are set, as is the decision to film one. And here's the thing, I've definitely been put forward for this new promotion. I thought everything had gone quiet on that front but I'm due for a whole battery of interviews. I must find out who else is up for this. The level grade is obviously higher as is the attendant salary increase, so fingers crossed please.

Yours as ever

Arthur Pendragon

82

From: Arthur Shilling [arthur.shilling@gammondhopes.com]
Sent: 09/8/2012 23.16 PM GMT
To: Steven Charteris [stevencharteris@staracademy.com]
Subject: Fim crews – yuch

Steven

I've had three meetings now with the film people who will be shooting the Chairman's Forum. They all seemed to be on drugs of some sort because I couldn't understand a word any of them were saying. The director was the least voluble and mumbled the whole way through. Eventually, I left the meeting room and went to see

Jez Staffordshire who couldn't have been less interested. Mr Bose, however, came back with me to the meeting room and made it very clear that either a) the crew could go now and we'd fire the agency or b) they could cut the crap and we'd have a proper conversation. The director started mumbling again and Mr Bose opened the meeting room door. As if by magic, English was spoken clearly and wisely. There was not one iota of embarrassment on the part of the creative bunch, but at least we had a conversation that led to an understanding of what the brief was.

I've had my first interview for the promotion. It was with Jez Staffordshire and, for some reason, Mr Goodenhardt. "Job interviews," said Mr G, "are critical to the quality of an organisation's people. OK?" He went on, "Good job interview processes and methods increase the quality of people in an organisation. Poor processes and methods result in poor selection, which undermines organisational capabilities, wastes management time and increases staff turnover. OK?" Mr G nodded in my direction as I sat bolt upright, unsure as to how I might respond. He drawled, "Interviews should not place undue pressure on interviewees, because people tend to withdraw and become defensive under pressure. We learn more about people when they relax. Are *you* relaxed?" There followed a wide selection of questions which one or the other of my two interviewers seemed to answer on my behalf. I left in something of a daze and noticed Jenny Barstiff waiting to go in. She's one of the competition!

Best to you and Mrs C. Hope she's feeling a bit better.

Arthur

83

From: Arthur Shilling [arthur.shilling@gammondhopes.com]
Sent: 09/10/2012 17.16 PM GMT
To: Steven Charteris [stevencharteris@staracademy.com]
Subject: In a hurry

Steven

Today is warm and full of early autumn smells. The day has been a good one. The film crew have put forward their plans for the Chairman's Forum shoot and everyone has agreed that they're fine and, as the director said, "doable". The Chairman's people seem pleased with the way things are going.

Chloe smiled at me this morning. Mrs Sourdough smiled at me and Mr Almoun not only smiled, but winked and shot me with his fingers – always a good sign. The only slight problem of the day was the wonky air conditioning on our floor. One minute we get great rushes of arctic ice – quite refreshing, although the ladies don't like it and resort to cardigan or sweatshirt donning, or we receive huge wafts of hot and fetid air. A giant with halitosis comes to mind.

I have to run now because I'm due to go for my second promotion interview in fifteen minutes. Wish me luck.

Arthur

84

From: Arthur Shilling [arthur.shilling@gammondhopes.com]
Sent: 09/12/2012 22.16 PM GMT
To: Steven Charteris [stevencharteris@staracademy.com]
Subject: Interviewed out

Steven

I don't believe it. Jenny Barstiff's got the promotion! Extraordinary. I met Mr Flattergleich coming out of a meeting room. He saw me and said, "I svair to Gott, Artur, I don't font hear it." Behind him was Mr Goodenhardt who stared at me coolly and said, "I saw you in *Twelfth Night*. Considering we had to pay for our seats, my wife and I did our best to appreciate the performance." They both nodded and were gone. I've put in all the hard graft. I've travelled the world on behalf of this rotten bank. I've put up with all the rubbish from my esteemed colleagues and have done more than my bit. This is the thanks I get!

Drink calls and I collected my pal Graham Graveling (he from the Shakedown Players and my best bud). We headed to a bar and after a couple of hours found ourselves in some altercation or other. An Irishman was arguing that Beckett was better than Shakespeare and that Seamus Heaney was better than William Blake. I put forward a case that Jonathan Swift was excellent and the man took offence because, he said, Swift wasn't properly Irish. He (the man not Swift) kept calling me "Me ole bucko" and then some time later confided, "Tis one more trink oim needn to take de toiredness from me ole boans. I desoives it. Diggin de spods in de mod from dawn till dork meks a man toisty." Then he laughed and said, "See you lads." Graham pointed out to me that the man was no more Irish than I and actually worked for GH and could be found on the 3rd floor in Trusts.

Arthur

85

From: Arthur Shilling [arthur.shilling@gammondhopes.com]
Sent: 09/13/2012 19.16 PM GMT
To: Steven Charteris [stevencharteris@staracademy.com]
Subject: The bowels of the earth

Steven

I still can't get over it. Jenny Barstiff got promoted. My landlady, the lovely Victoria, has tried to perk me up a bit and has been all smiles and sorrowful gazes. Chloe clasped me by the shoulders and shook her head saying, "It's OK Arthur, you'll get there." I think she made my nose bleed a little. Of Mr Bose there's no sign – special project I suppose. Mrs Sourdough said, "We can't all be the boss or some such thing, you know, Arthur."

Drink calls again, but a lonely bar stool this time. I have no need of company and would make a poor companion.

Arthur (the lush) Shilling

86

From: Arthur Shilling [arthur.shilling@gammondhopes.com]
Sent: 09/15/2012 22.16 PM GMT
To: Steven Charteris [stevencharteris@staracademy.com]
Subject: A talking to

Steven

Mr Bose has spent an hour or so talking to me and saying that I should brush the disappointment away and move on. He said that I'm doing a good job and that I am well regarded. My head hung in shame and I found it hard to look him in the eye. He asked me if I liked rock and roll. Surprised, I said yes and he handed me two tickets for a one-off concert of my favourite band in the whole world at The O2! "Wow!" I said, "Thanks Mr Bose." Then he told me about promotion interviews.

"A promotion interview, Arthur, is about climbing the ladder, without changing the wall it is up against," began Mr B. "After all you don't necessarily have to move on, in order to move up." He paused and looked out of the window. I could see a certain sadness on his kind face. He tapped the table with his usual staccato beat and I knew better than to interrupt. "If you're preparing for a job promotion interview you must see your future growth linked to that of the organisation. That's an obvious but important thing. Many people waste their careers and lives in organisations that don't fit them, so finding the right match for you is no mean feat. But you do fit in here, Arthur, despite the one or two setbacks you've had. We all have those." Again he paused and looked away.

"You're an insider now, Arthur. You understand the role of the different cogs that comprise the organisational machine. You have access to information and knowledge an external candidate could only dream of. Plus you know how to get hold of the things you don't know. You know and understand the company culture and you understand what is important to success within the organisation and what it takes to fit in. It's just that this role suited Jenny better than it did you and, despite what you may think, she's worked hard and has developed hugely. You've ignored her because you think that she's just silly and an airhead, had a fling with a senior executive and dances a great deal. But, she's good. If you want the part, you better work for it. Prepare. Think of the next opportunity as you would an audition. Remember the perception of you is constantly being shaped. Look like a person who's ready to take the next step up. Attitude is important. Look and sound as though you are ready for bigger things and you'll find bigger things come to you."

I recall the meeting with Mr B almost verbatim because he meant every word and he speaks beautifully. Once he'd finished his chat, he looked at me for a moment, pocketed his silver pencil that he'd used as a drum stick and left the room.

Drink calls.

Arthur

87

From: Arthur Shilling [arthur.shilling@gammondhopes.com]
Sent: 09/20/2012 04.16 AM GMT
To: Steven Charteris [stevencharteris@staracademy.com]
Subject: A bit better

Steven

I've had a few hangovers over the last few days and feel terrible. My landlady, Victoria Holyhead, was quite cross with me and told me to get a bloody grip. Mrs Sourdough has given me some brown liquid in a small bottle that she says will have me right in no time. I discharged the liquid down the sink in the gentlemen's washroom much to the interest of Mr Chesney Bluesnip, who works in Overseas Deposits on the 27th floor. He looked at me quizzically but I was in no mood for idle banter. He looked away and anyway he had other matters to which he needed to attend, having just splashed water from the tap all over the front of his light grey trousers.

I've thought long and hard about what Mr Bose said and have considered other careers: the French Foreign Legion being one attractive option. Another is the Navy. There are many Shillings in the Royal Navy's history although my sailing is limited given that I suffer dreadfully from seasickness. I also discovered that I'm not a Pendragon, not even a Dragon never mind the Pen bit and my connection with the Arthurian Legend is nil.

Drink is the only answer.

Arthur

88

From: Arthur Shilling [arthur.shilling@gammondhopes.com]
Sent: 09/22/2012 13.16 PM GMT
To: Steven Charteris [stevencharteris@staracademy.com]
Subject: Better!

Dear Steven

Better. Mr F and Jenny B had really good chats with me and I feel much, much happier. I bear Jenny no ill will and indeed wished her well. She gave me a hug. The drink is no more and I'm throwing myself back into the fray. The Foreign Legion application form is in the bin and the Navy will have to manage without this Shilling.

Preparations for the Chairman's Forum in London are well under way with a fair amount of catching up on my part. Dephne Hong has been understanding, but now I "must focus", she said. Mr Bose caught my eye this morning and smiled. The date of the concert for which he gave me tickets is coming up and I must decide whom I should take. Chloe? Landlady with the red hair? Mrs Sourdough?

Please do thank Mrs C for sending me the colon cleansing kit – which caused me much embarrassment at the office and mirth amongst my colleagues. I can't see how the apparatus would help my low spirits, but hey. And why did she send it to the office for goodness' sake? I'll return the gift if I may and perhaps Mrs C could get her money back?

Arthur

89

From: Arthur Shilling [arthur.shilling@gammondhopes.com]
Sent: 09/27/2012 12.16 PM GMT
To: Steven Charteris [stevencharteris@staracademy.com]
Subject: The London Forum

Dear Steven

The Chairman's Forum went really well. We had some of the regular contributors and speakers along with a number of fresh and untried faces. Some said that this was a risky move but I did a great deal of research into each person's background, track record and ability to deliver. We also tried a new facilitator, someone who had been introduced to me in Dubai. She's a well known broadcaster for CNN and has undertaken similar tasks for other multinational businesses. She was excellent, although one of her high heels in show two became stuck as she stepped up on stage for the first time. She didn't panic but just said, "Arthur, would you mind…?" And I, sitting on the end of the front row with earphones clamped to my head listening to all of the showcaller's instructions, immediately leapt up, hurt my ears badly because I hadn't removed said earphones and rushed to aid the damsel in distress. All was freed and no damage caused to shoes or facilitator. Some in the audience dared a giggle or two but the Chairman, sitting next to me, half rose and turned his head. All giggling ceased forthwith.

The Chairman is still never sure of my name, but knows who I am and more or less what I do. He's grateful for some script inputs and dismissive of others. I'm slightly nervous of addressing him or asking him anything because he's a bit like royalty and normally you have to go through serried ranks to get an answer to the simplest of questions. Occasionally he asks an aide a question who might tiptoe across to me for the answer.

I had suggested that we use someone who could write down the highlights of the event, transpose said highlights into mini-newspaper format and have said document in delegates' hands within hours. Mr F thought the idea excellent and I found an ex-deputy editor of a major international journal who's reliable, intelligent and very helpful. He's part of the Forum team now and worth every penny.

The video people did their job well too in the end – despite the mumbling episode. The finished programme of the event hasn't been fully edited so judgement is reserved. The director seemed to speak perfectly clearly throughout the shoot and was very polite to everyone.

More auditions! Of Shakespeare's 37 plays, *Richard III* isn't the one I'd have picked for our motley crew, but there you are. I will I think throw caution to the wind and audition for the title role. I have practised the "My horse, my horse…" speech *ad infinitum* and can walk as if my hunchback is painful and has caused my anger and nastiness.

Must run. It's rock and roll tonight and Mr Bose's tickets!

Arthur Hendrix

90

From: Arthur Shilling [arthur.shilling@gammondhopes.com]
Sent: 10/01/2012 23.16 PM GMT
To: Steven Charteris [stevencharteris@staracademy.com]
Subject: "Now go we in content. To liberty and not to banishment."

Steve

I used the above quote (obviously *As You Like It* Act I, scene iii) because Celia speaks these words to her cousin and good friend, Rosalind, as they prepare to be 'banished' from the court to the country. Unfortunately we have here a banishment and not an open door to liberty. Jez Staffordshire has been asked to resign! Nobody's sure precisely why, but rumours fly hither and thither. One minute he was wobbling about the place, pleasant enough – the next minute, i.e. today, gone!

The rock concert ('gig') was brilliant and I have another surprise for you. Jenny (for she was my guest) and I turned up quite early and were pleased just to absorb the atmosphere and watch the two support bands. The first was really poor. But, the second was very good and slightly redolent of a middle-years Pink Floyd. I was about to get refreshments for dear Jenny when something odd caught my eye. The band's drummer was drumming in a particular way that rang a bell. We were too far back to see the stage properly but I looked closely at the huge screens. When the cameras picked up the drummer the focus was mostly on his drumming and not on his face. But, suddenly there was a close up and I staggered back, treading heavily on a mature lady's bunioned foot. "Oy, watch it you stupid idiot!" she yelled, spraying me with breadcrumbs and beer. I apologised profusely and looked back at the screens – but that had been the band's last number and they were walking off stage. I racked my brains because, without doubt, I knew the drummer.

Jenny is a peach and she even gave me a peck on the cheek when I delivered her safely back to Shepherd's Bush.

Mr Rolling Arthur Stones

>

From: Steven Charteris [stevencharteris@staracademy.com]
Sent:10/07/2012 07.00 AM GMT
To: Arthur Shilling [arthur.shilling@gammondhopes.com]
Subject: Onwards

Dear Arthur

We were very troubled by the fact that you had slipped so low to the depths of despair and I very nearly got myself a ticket for the 09.13 non-stop to London to be with you in your hour of need. I'm glad that you've bucked up now. Mrs C really only meant for the best when she considered your colon the root of the overall problem. There was no need to return the equipment – albeit a kind thought on your part.

You will, in the course of your career, find obstacles and a bumpy road from time to time. There will be disappointments, some of them large and some of them huge. There will be times when you believe that life is totally unfair and unreasonable. You will discover that those you consider less able will get promoted over your head or get the Shakespearean part that you felt to be your own. (By the way, don't you think that Richard might be a tad ambitious? I mean this kindly – but perhaps something more modest would suit your talents? I do so well remember your Fool from *King Lear*.)

Disappointments come in battalions, others come singly. But they exist for everyone, although some more so than others. You have to learn how to cope with upsets and, in time, you will.

Promotion interviews

- Applying for an internal promotion can be a nerve-wracking experience. Not only do you have to undergo the intensive selection process with colleagues or external candidates but, as an existing employee, your employer will already have experience of your strengths and weaknesses.

- If you feel confident that you can do the job well and you have appropriate experience, then you are already halfway there. The second step is to ensure that you have prepared thoroughly before you attend your interview or interviews. Although these are internal, you must treat them as any other job interview because your assessors will compare your experience, skill set and attitude with other candidates. So, while you may believe that you are the best for the job, do not assume that your employers will just give you the job because you work for them and know them.

- Be aware that not everyone will like you in life and neither will you like everyone. People form impressions of others very quickly and one small thing can colour a view forever. That's the way it is.

- Try to find out as much as you can about the job, including:
  - the extent of the duties and relationships,
  - the history, expectations and the reasons why this role has become vacant,
  - the reason this position has been created.

- It's also about time that you perhaps patched up any weak areas in your knowledge about the company and its structure and services. You may need to ask colleagues about unfamiliar areas of the business or company history so that you maximise the competitive edge you have over other candidates and feel confident going in to your interview.

- Try to anticipate the sorts of questions you're likely to be asked by your interviewers and prepare answers carefully. Self-assessment will help you to think about why you have been included among the candidates. Think of experience and skills that illustrate how you are qualified for your next role. It's essential that you provide information about the impact you have had on the business and your commitment to achieving longer term aims; you need to demonstrate how your career has developed within the organisation.

- With interviews, take time to answer questions and give concise answers. Try to keep relaxed and think positively, end on an optimistic note and deal with the closing moments particularly well. Do not assume that the interviewers are aware of the specifics of your current role and ensure you highlight your personal strengths clearly.

- If you are selected for promotion, you will have new challenges and possibly a different team to work with so

make sure you ask relevant questions about the position, for example:
- what would your new responsibilities be?
- what are the likely challenges?
- what sort of support can you expect?
- to whom will you report?
- what development opportunities exist?
- what is the grade/pay?
- what are the differences to your current contract?

- Finally, Arthur, if you are not selected for promotion, ask for feedback. Perhaps with regard to your recent experience, your interview technique let you down or maybe your employers felt that there are some skills you might not currently have. Perhaps you were over-confident.

Your drinking worried me and you know full well the history of the Charteris household, so I just urge you to some caution. I'm delighted that Mr Bose talked to you in the way he did and, as ever, offered sensible counsel. I'd quite like to meet him one day – perhaps when we come down and see your next crack at Shakespeare and I promise you we will.

For now, take care

Steven Charteris

Chapter Ten

"Our revels now are ended. These our actors,
As I foretold you, were all spirits, and
Are melted into air, into thin air:
And like the baseless fabric of this vision,
The cloud-capp'd tow'rs, the gorgeous palaces,
The solemn temples, the great globe itself,
Yea, all which it inherit, shall dissolve,
And, like this insubstantial pageant faded,
Leave not a rack behind. We are such stuff
As dreams are made on; and our little life
Is rounded with a sleep."

Prospero: *The Tempest* (IV, i)

91

From: Arthur Shilling [arthur.shilling@gammondhopes.com]
Sent: 10/29/2012 15.16 PM GMT
To: Steven Charteris [stevencharteris@staracademy.com]
Subject: Jours française

Dear Steven

Forgive the tardiness of my reply to your latest mail for which ever thanks, but I was asked to join Jenny and her family in France for a few days and I decided, as did she, that we'd forget work for a while. While we are genuinely just 'good friends', St Paul de Vence, where her parents had rented a house, was very romantic. The village is on a charming hilltop in Provence, filled with marvellous little art galleries, boutiques and cafés. And winding streets, elegant fountains, vine-covered stone walls and statues tucked into nooks in the walls. Breathtaking views of mountains and sea. Mrs Barstiff is an excellent cook and Mr Barstiff is a dab hand at barbecues. I was allowed to enjoy good food, excellent wines, fun company and a wallow in the salt water swimming pool.

There was one slightly embarrassing moment when I was taking the family out for dinner one evening as a 'thank you' and who should walk in but our Deputy Chairman and his wife. Well, I *assume* that she was his wife – certainly very glamorous and much younger than him. As they say here, '*à chacun son goût*' and I must admit his taste was/is very good. He couldn't avoid us really, since the restaurant was so small, so I had to stand up along with Jenny to introduce everyone. He of course couldn't remember my name or Jenny's and there was that awkward pause when nobody quite knows what to say or do. His creaking gate voice was much the same and, later, when he spoke risible French, you could see the waiters and sommelier flinch.

Now I'm back and hungry for action. There are still rumours flying about the reasons for Jez Staffordshire's departure. Mr Almoun held a meeting at which he said that there would be some changes but he refused to comment on the reasons for Jez's resignation. I asked Mr Bose if I might have Jez's home address because I wanted to send a card, but Mr B said that Jez had left the country! I tried his mobile but it was an office BlackBerry and had been shut down.

I have to turn my attention to the Chairman's Forum video edit which is late in its completion – partly my fault. But the Chairman's office is keen to see the finished product so off I go to darkest Soho.

Arthur

92

From: Arthur Shilling [arthur.shilling@gammondhopes.com]
Sent: 11/05/2012 02.16 AM GMT
To: Steven Charteris [stevencharteris@staracademy.com]
Subject: Video edits and, *ay caramba*, other matters

Steven

I bumped into your English department's Professor Franklin this morning as I was walking down Wardour Street to the video edit suite. She was on her way to some conference or other; 'TS Eliot and His Fevered Brow' I think the subject was. Prof Franklin was full of beans – literally, since she'd just had a big fry up at an Italian café in Frith Street. She did say that Mrs C had had been accused of taking a toothbrush from a high street store without paying. I am sorry that it has come to this and I can only express my sorrow. Hard times.

My rehearsals for *Richard III* have begun. Our lisping friend got the lead and Jenny is playing Lady Anne, a small but tender part. I was trying to explain the characters to Mrs Sourdough. She just stared blankly at me and, popping a throat lozenge into her ruby-lipped mouth, said that *EastEnders* was more her thing. As for me, I am playing Buckingham. I think you were right about Richard and I like the idea of playing Richard's ruthless, right-hand man helping him to gain power. Buckingham is almost as amoral and ambitious as Richard himself so I have some good material with which to play. Now that our esteemed director, Ms Nookles, has decided that the comedic route is wrong, I will make myself evil incarnate. Apparently I worried everyone in the lift yesterday because I was trying out terrifying faces in the mirror. Mr Alan Trebbish came up to have a word.

Video editing is not very exciting. The mumbling director was there when I arrived this morning, although he was a touch more explicit. As John of Gaunt says in *Richard II* (II, i), "Where words are scarce, they are seldom spent in vain." But sometimes I'm not so sure.

Dephne Hong was there too and hitting the Coca-Cola hard. She looked bored too, but smiled at me and patted the seat next to her. By lunchtime my eyes were glazing and the morning's lustre had worn off. After lunch (comprising of the biggest and fattest sandwich I'd ever seen, causing bits of tomato and lettuce to fall none-too-gracefully to the floor), the Chairman's PA arrived to look at how our hard work was going. He seemed satisfied, made two succinct suggestions which brooked little argument and left. Dephne seemed satisfied and she left too, but I had to stay until nine o'clock this evening to ensure that everything was finished properly. Dephne had made me promise to see through the final 'cut' three times to check for errors and I did just that. The editor seemed pleased that I was pleased.

As I was walking to Tottenham Court Road Underground, I heard some really good music coming from a rehearsal studio in the lofty heights of a trendy building. I went closer because I recognised the music – a mix between The Killers and the solo offering from Brendon Flowers with a hint of Pink Floyd in the post Roger Waters days. I went to the door and asked who was rehearsing. I asked if I could just have a peep and the security guy naturally shook his head but, just then, there was an altercation in the street and he went to investigate. I sneaked in to the studio reception and ran up the stairs. The music had stopped and I suddenly felt very foolish because one of the studio doors was pushed open and out came the band members, including the one I had been expecting –

Mr Bose! He was in the middle of sharing a joke with a very pretty lady and then he saw me and his face froze for a moment. "You've found me out Arthur. Found me out." Then he grinned, put an arm round my shoulders and said, "We're going for something to eat. Want to join us?" Well, of course I did.

Best

Arthur

93

From: Arthur Shilling [arthur.shilling@gammondhopes.com]
Sent: 11/7/2012 20.16 PM GMT
To: Steven Charteris [stevencharteris@staracademy.com]
Subject: "Be not afeard…"

Steven

"Be not afeard.
The isle is full of noises,
Sounds, and sweet airs, that give delight and hurt not.
Sometimes a thousand twangling instruments
Will hum about mine ears…"

Mr Bose quoted Taliban (one of your favourite *Tempest* quotations as I recall) at our dinner and I was amazed to discover that he had studied Shakespeare! He was very warm in his explanation of his part-time membership of an amazing rock band. He didn't ask me to keep the matter to myself, but I will and he knows it. Apparently he's always been in bands and once seriously considered taking it up full-time. He had a drum set when he was seven and hasn't really looked back since. He lives with his sister and has never married, although he's had opportunities he said. During dinner he did look quite longingly at Trudy, the lady with the lovely smile who plays lead guitar in the band. During the day she works for a large international publishing firm and is heavily into Shakespeare too!

The Chairman's Forum video edit was completed and the result was given the thumbs up. Mr Rattles came up to my desk and said, "Well done, Arthur. I have some notes for you that you may care to see on the matter of video production." "Thank you," said I and meant it. Deaf Knee said that Mr Michael Evington, our Group CEO, whom we never see much because he's based in Hong Kong, was thinking of doing a world roadshow and presenting his vision and Group plans to as many bank people as possible. Would I be interested in being on the roadshow team? Would I?!

As good as his word, Derek Rattles sent me an email with the following and very useful advice:

From: Derek Rattles [derek.j.d.rattles@gammondhopes.com]
Sent: 11/8/2012 07.16 AM GMT
To: Arthur Shilling [arthur.shilling@gammondhopes.com]
Subject: Video production can be the bane of our lives

Arthur

Remind me to tell you about the mixed-up reel incident when a reel of film (way back in the old days circa 1986) fell off the back of a motorcycle, was found and then my assistant took it on the Underground where the magnets from the electric motors wiped the thing clean! The film was meant to be about our then new ATM machines but of course a huge chunk of film was missing which would have been impossible to reshoot. So I got my friend, a presenter at a Manchester TV studio to do a talking head piece that lasted a good 20 minutes to bridge the two parts of the film that we still had. The finished thing won no awards and I wasn't promoted for another two years.

Given your more recent experience with production people and post-production, here are some further thoughts that might assist:

- When commissioning a video or film, it's easy for corporate organisations to forget that material from movies, TV and the world of music all need permission or licenses. And both come at a price. If in doubt get independent advice – I can certainly help here as can Sheila Shenanigans, or whatever her name is, in Legal. She's very good.

- Be wary of production companies that say something like, "We do a bit of everything – websites, PR, graphic design, events, print… oh and video." A good rule of thumb is that if the number of services offered by a company is greater than the number of employees, you might want to consider getting another quote. Same applies to any supplier of communication services.

- By the way, creating video for the web is not the same as creating video for broadcast, entertainment or presentation at an event. Viewing behaviours are very different online. You also have to consider delivery platforms, hosting options, interactivity, conversion techniques, social media aspects of your video and many other factors unique to web use. You must always consult real experts.

- The MD of a video company I know once said, allegedly off the record, "We just do corporate video to pay the bills, but we'd much rather be doing television." I suppose his comment was refreshingly honest. Unless a video production company you've hired is working under the direction of an ad agency or similar or they specialise in the type of video programmes *you* want, you shouldn't be surprised if the resulting video is wonderfully irrelevant.

- If you're not comfortable with a member of the team provided by your agency, then say so. If you have good reasons and even if you just feel uncomfortable, do something. If everything else fails come and have a word with me or Hermann or Mr Bose. (*Entres nous*, perhaps not Mr Goodenhardt.)

- In my (limited) experience, corporate video objectives are sometimes loose or wide. Mark Twain wrote, "I'm sorry I wrote you such a long letter but I didn't have time to write a short one." It's really difficult to be succinct. It also seems risky. Script-by-committee is death to most video projects. In video, shorter is almost always better. Look at good TV commercials. They have one message, one proposition and they make their point quickly and, usually, successfully. Just like a commercial, a video programme has to communicate a message or convince people of something. Make a programme that will work for the end-audience.

- The best messages work on a visceral level. They make you think; more so, they make you *feel* something. It's also much better to show people things – don't just *tell* them. Facts are important, but a good story is better. Put the facts into the story. How do you find a company with this type of experience? Look at their previous video work. If it's not engaging, yours won't be either.

- Too often, videos are created in isolation. Our brand (and indeed any brand) is the sum total of all of the experiences people have with our company and that includes video. Video production is not an isolated activity. Neither is an event, a piece of print, an inclusion on a website. So many pieces of communication are executed without reference to an organisation's tone of voice, design, brand, vocabulary, and even colours and fonts. I refer you to that brochure that Trusts produced last month!

- As with any piece of communication, it's critical to decide what we want people to do *after* they have watched our/your video programme. If *you* don't know, your viewer won't either.

By the by, Arthur, reports about your progress are all positive, so well done.

Well, Steven, I was very pleased with that. Mr Derek R has rarely been so voluble so perhaps he sees me as part of the 'squad'. *Je suis arrivé!*

By the way, big news. My landlady, she with the shining red hair, the delicious Victoria Holyhead, has announced that she's getting married and she has given me notice to leave my accommodation. I didn't even know there was a significant other. I have three months to find somewhere else. But where?

Have just inadvertently deleted all of the Chairman's Forum photographs – genuine error and clumsy old me. Hopefully nobody will want any pictures now that the event has been done and dusted.

Just had an email from the Chairman's office to say that the Chairman sends his compliments and would much like us to produce a coffee table book utilising the photographs from all the Forum events – or words to that effect. Oh my giddy aunt!

Trembling… and yet strangely composed.

Arthur

94

From: Arthur Shilling [arthur.shilling@gammondhopes.com]
Sent: 11/11/2012 20.16 PM GMT
To: Steven Charteris [stevencharteris@staracademy.com]
Subject: Relief and a surprise

Steven

Well, retrieving the photographs was no easy task but, with the help of three wise chaps from the IT department, the task was managed. Huge sigh of relief on my part and promises of quantities of beer for the IT people. Mr Goodenhardt today announced that he thinks that the book idea is a waste of time and money, so now the book plan is on permanent hold. I am calm. Mr Almoun said, "You're very calm in the circs. You OK?" I told him I was fine thank you. On my desk discovered an envelope with a CD and a card with a short note from Mr Bose saying: 'Thought you might like to have a listen.' And written on the other side:

"The man that hath no music in himself,
Nor is not mov'd with concord of sweet sounds,
Is fit for treasons, stratagems, and spoils."

Lorenzo: *The Merchant of Venice* (V, i)

Mr Bose was not in again today and Mrs Sourdough says that he isn't well. I have no idea where he lives and his mobile remains unanswered. I sent him a get well email.

Arthur

95

From: Arthur Shilling [arthur.shilling@gammondhopes.com]
Sent: 11/14/2012 23.16 PM GMT
To: Steven Charteris [stevencharteris@staracademy.com]
Subject: The world is changing

Steven

The CEO's world roadshow is definitely going to happen! Dephne Hong has officially asked Mr F if I can be a permanent member of her team! Mr F is considering the situation and has asked to see me tomorrow. Mr Rattles smiled at me in the lift. I thanked him for his video email and he said, "*de nada*". His wife's Spanish apparently or he goes to Spain for his holidays – something like that.

Still no news of Mr Bose. I haven't really talked to him about his music and his band. I'd really like to hear them play again and I have loads of questions about the what, how and when. And if. The CD of his music is amazing.

Had an email (not just to me but to about a hundred thousand people) from Jez Staffordshire to say that he was in the Cayman Islands working for a small financial services 'operation'. Not sure what an FS 'operation' is and neither does anyone else, but we all think that it's perhaps not legitimate. Mr S made no mention of why he left in such a hurry, but he sounded happy enough and he sent an attachment which was a photo of the beach (allegedly) as seen from his bedroom window. Could be a prison cell window for all we know.

Jenny Barstiff and I still see each other a fair amount, particularly at our *Richard III* rehearsals. I am hugely villainous in my character although the director has asked me to tone it down because a) Richard III has complained that I'm overshadowing his nastiness and b) there are likely to be school children in the audience and we don't want them to rush out of the auditorium screaming, do we? At rehearsals now I tend not to answer to the name Arthur, but will only respond if I am addressed as Buckingham or m'Lord. Two people in the cast (very small bit players I should add) have threatened to beat the living daylights out of me if I don't stop being so stupid. Graham Graveling, my best pal, came up to have a serious word or two. Even Jenny told me to stop being a plonker. It really wasn't like this in the Dotheby Players, was it Professor?

I had an email from Josh Stonewall, the General Manager from New York. He's coming over to the UK and wants to meet and 'catch up'. Well, well. I also had an email from Gloria Mishmash from PR wanting to know if I'd like to partner her to some annual dinner dance thing. Black tie, awards, some terrible comedian, warm champagne... but still. Hmmm well, well, well. My cup runneth over. And there's more. Dephne Hong sent me an email saying that the CEO of the Private Bank was definitely going ahead with his Customer Congress event in Monaco and the Swedish lady (large yet munchkin-like if you recall) whom I met way back and her odd Australian colleague wanted me to be involved!

I do actually think that I'm related to the Buckingham family. George Villiers, Earl of Buckingham, became the favourite of James I after they first met in 1614. Villiers had come from humble stock and my father's family had a Villiers in it centuries ago. And we're humble. In 1620, Buckingham married Lady Catherine Manners, the daughter of the Duke of Rutland. My mother apparently had a Manners in the family back in the mist of time. And she's certainly humble too.

I hope that Mrs C is improving.

Buckingham

96

From: Arthur Shilling [arthur.shilling@gammondhopes.com]
Sent: 11/20/2012 22.16 PM GMT
To: Steven Charteris [stevencharteris@staracademy.com]
Subject: The world turns

Steven

I have to write a speech for Mr Frattergleich – overnight! He's been asked out of the blue to be the host at a dinner for people in the bank who have done something special over and above the call of duty. The scheme's been around for a while, but so far it's always been managed by PR. Now it's come into our world.

Mr F asked me for various bits of advice about the evening and then said that, if I was going to join Dephne Hong's team, the least I could do was to help him with this 'gig' as he put it! Not sure what to think. Of course I said that I'd help in any way I could and he said, "Vell I neet a speech to show Zair Chriztopher tomorrow so... here are my nodes und ze brief. OK?" Then, do you know what, he winked. He's never done that before ever and that's always been the domain of Mr Almoun.

Still no sign of Mr Bose.

Best

Buckingham

97

From: Arthur Shilling [arthur.shilling@gammondhopes.com]
Sent: 11/23/2012 22.16 PM GMT
To: Steven Charteris [stevencharteris@staracademy.com]
Subject: Wow

Steven

Mr F had prepared an excellent brief for his speech (as always) and in turn I prepared a good speech (even though I say so myself) for him. Mrs Sourdough somehow got hold of a copy and said that it made her cry! Well, the event *is* all about helping old ladies across the road, walking through storms to deliver a five pound note or going to the North Pole to fill an ATM machine out of office hours. Stuff like that. Mr F said that the Chairman's PA was impressed and he doesn't impress easily (or at all). Mr F also winked at me this morning as we passed each other en route for coffee. I wondered if he had something in his eye.

But here's the best news – I had an interview this morning for the new post of Senior Events' Executive and I got the job! More money – yey. I took all of your advice and that of Mr Bose, prepared myself properly and did my homework. I'll be on the same team as Jenny and now we're the same grade or 'grate' as Mr F calls it. I have to move to a different floor and my role will be to support all the Group's very senior executive events.

Mr Almoun comes round less frequently now but, when he does, he still winks and shoots me with a finger gun. Yesterday I 'shot' him back and he fell to the ground rolling round in pretend agony. How we laughed the laugh of the criminally insane until Mr Rattles enquired as to whether we were *compos mentis* and running a bank or a kindergarten. Mr Almoun was laughing so much that stuff that normally should remain in the nose (or deposited into a paper handkerchief and flushed down the toilet) shot out all over his shirt. He had to borrow a handkerchief (mine) which wasn't returned (thankfully).

Best, as ever to you both. Will you come to London and see *Richard III*? Please do say that you will.

I have discovered that I am of no relation to anyone called Villiers, Manners or Buckingham.

Arthur Shilling

98

From: Arthur Shilling [arthur.shilling@gammondhopes.com]
Sent: 11/26/2012 23.16 PM GMT
To: Steven Charteris [stevencharteris@staracademy.com]
Subject: Mr Bose

Steven

Mr Bose has died. I can't believe it. We were told this morning and everyone was just stunned. Apparently he had been ill for a long time, but had said nothing to anyone. I have to admit to being tearful and had to leave the office at lunchtime. Walked and walked. Ended up in Soho where I'd heard his band play. Am at a loss really. I miss him and wanted to be his friend. I only knew him a little but liked him a lot. Someone once said that good people are scarce and he was a good man, a decent man. I miss him more than I can say and I looked across today at where he used to sit, leaning as far back as his chair would allow. Or drumming on the desk with a pencil while he was thinking. The times that he helped me, gently putting me right where I had clearly gone wrong and metaphorically patting me on the back when I had got things right. I don't quite know what to do.

Arthur

99

From: Arthur Shilling [arthur.shilling@gammondhopes.com]
Sent: 11/28/2012 21.16 PM GMT
To: Steven Charteris [stevencharteris@staracademy.com]
Subject: Ms Bose

Steven

The funeral was a plain affair. Funnily enough, Mr Bose was Jewish. I had no idea, him being from India originally. His sister was just like him, with a warm, kindly face and a gentle smile. She knew who I was once I mentioned my name and took my hands in hers. I couldn't see properly, much less speak. Stood there looking silly I suppose. I wanted to say something to her but I could only mutter something inane.

The small chapel was full to bursting with a mixture of banking people and rock 'n' roll folk. I expected the whole thing to be sombre and to begin with it was, but there suddenly burst forth from the speakers a mix of heavy rock followed by some gentle classical guitar – Julian Bream I think. There didn't seem to be many from Mr Bose's family – just a small number – but loads of friends. Our whole department was there and many from other parts of the bank and indeed other banks.

Most of the service was phonetically set out for us and we all followed it the best we could. When it came for the most sacred prayer for the dead we were all weeping. It begins: "*Yitgaddal veyitqaddash shmeh rabba*" ("May His great name be exalted and sanctified") and was read beautifully by Mr Bose's lady friend and band member, Trudy. One of Mr Bose's other friends from the band gave a eulogy and by this time poor Mr F and most of the people I had grown to like and trust over the last year or so were crying. Jenny held my hand and I held Mrs Sourdough's. When we walked out to the grave led by the rabbi and Mr Bose's sister, I realised that until today I never knew Mr Bose's first name.

I did think about not continuing with *Richard III* and last night was the first performance. However, I did do it of course and that's what Mr B would have wanted. He was with me in a funny sort of way. Do you know what I mean, Professor? Do you? And apparently he'd been to every one of my performances. I had to really get a grip because a crying and red-eyed Buckingham would be no good and not at all ferocious. A kingmaker doesn't weep, not in public anyhow. I got through the play and the director said that it was a moving performance. Graham gave me a hug. I went straight home. Victoria Holyhead was out – probably with her new beau and the house was very empty. I sat in the dark in my room.

I'm due to start my new job in the next few days and I'm sort of looking forward to that.

I hope you are well and Mrs C. Don't worry about not coming to see the play. I understand.

Best

Arthur Shilling

100

From: Arthur Shilling [arthur.shilling@gammondhopes.com]
Sent: 12/10/2012 23.16 PM GMT
To: Steven Charteris [stevencharteris@staracademy.com]
Subject: Away we go

Steven

This morning I began my new duties on the 29th floor. I now have a bigger desk and it's right next to Dephne Hong's office and very close to Jenny's. She has just told me that she's off to the States in a few months. Another promotion.

I apparently look blank and a bit zonked and spaced out from time to time, so I need to gather myself up a bit. I think about Mr B a lot. Whenever I do something at the moment – workwise certainly – I wonder what Mr B would have done. Or said.

Preparations are already fairly advanced for the CEO's world roadshow. I'm spending some time with an external logistics specialist planner who is sorting out the tour's route and venues. Her name is Evelyn Cocoteronne. She's of Italian descent and with parents who are also in the events business. She's calm and quietly gets on with the job in hand, although she can be forceful as I discovered when some hapless manager at some Athenian hotel was being more than usually flippant or lazy or both.

Our CEO is brisk and demanding. He knows precisely why he wants to do this tour but insists that us lower mortals put it into words, a job that's fallen to me. Not easy because he gives away few clues and his acolytes don't help but simper and grovel instead. Do you remember that chap who was in the Dotheby Players back in the day? What was his name? Ah, yes, Brian Hosegarden. You were on a sabbatical and he'd taken over for a while. Well, he always expected everyone to understand his intent and meaning when he was directing *Measure for Measure*. His notes post-rehearsal took up more time than the rehearsals themselves. I can remember him now: "For those who must stride across the stage in manner thus," and then he would describe the stride for ten minutes, "will find me a casual viewer and one who will not attend to the words that you have just spake. I would also consider it an honour Mr Shilling, if Isabella, a virtuous and chaste young woman, is allowed to show her emotion when faced with a hard decision when her brother is sentenced to death for unlawful sex. Standing in front of her simply will not do. It is her scene. And yes, I do know that Isabella does not approve of her brother's actions, but when she pleads for his life out of sisterly devotion, please Mr Shilling don't mouth the words along with her. It's disturbing. No, Mr Shilling I have never been a nun."

Our producer barely stopped for breath and on that occasion, if memory serves, he just went on, "You will all note, once more, that The Duke is central, central to the play. If anyone asks me again why he is dressed as a friar I will resign. Yes, Mr Shilling I am aware thank you. Yes, he does that so that he can observe.

Observe. Will *you* all observe? The Duke is unfailingly virtuous, good and kind-hearted. Can I remind all of you that Angelo is the villain of the play, a man who rules strictly and without mercy? No, his is not a comedic role, Mr Shilling. Now, if we're all ready, can we take Act IV from the top?" Ah, wonderful, heady days but we move on. Indeed we do.

I still see a fair bit of the old gang: Mrs Sourdough, Derek Rattles, Hermann Flattergleich (who's moving on to become General Manager of our Group Insurance operations in the Far East), Jeff Goodenhardt (who, at last, has got Mr F's old job) and Mr Khalif Almoun for whom I have a lot of affection and who gave me a big hug yesterday right in the middle of a crowded lift. I didn't care and hugged him right back. He still shoots me with his fingers when we meet in a corridor. Then he will just twirl like a ballet dancer (only a touch less gallant and graceful) and, bent low, will rush off weaving around people as they gaze on in astonishment.

I heard from Zalautha Derong, who is doing very well in Africa and has asked me to visit. But of Jez Staffordshire nobody has heard more. I hope that he is OK. And not in prison.

I think that I might stop our email correspondence for a while. I hope you won't be offended. It's not for any other reason than I don't want to keep burdening you with my worries and I suspect that you might have been a bit bored with all my tittle tattle. Suffice to say, let's see what the next few months bring and perhaps, if I may, I'll begin the process again. Of course, I would like very much to stay in touch and hope that we might speak on the phone from time to time. Your help has been extraordinary and I shall be ever grateful.

I miss you and I miss Mr Bose.

Do please give my very best to Mrs C and thank her for her lovely card. The marzipan has mostly fallen off as have the small animal figures, but the wool still remains – although that's frayed. It's a big card isn't it? But the idea was a good one and I shall keep it. I might get it framed and put it on my desk, next to the framed stubs of the The O2 concert tickets that Mr B gave me.

Fond regards as ever, Professor. And thank you.

Arthur Shilling

PS. I (really) understand what Brutus meant now:

"There is a tide in the affairs of men.
Which, taken at the flood, leads on to fortune;
Omitted, all the voyage of their life
Is bound in shallows and in miseries.
On such a full sea are we now afloat,
And we must take the current when it serves,
Or lose our ventures."

And this, read out by Mr Bose's sister at the funeral:

"Be not afeard.
The isle is full of noises,
Sounds, and sweet airs, that give delight and hurt not.
Sometimes a thousand twangling instruments
Will hum about mine ears; and sometime voices
That if I then had waked after long sleep
Will make me sleep again; and then, in dreaming

The clouds methought would open and show riches
Ready to drop upon me, that, when I waked,
I cried to dream again."

And, finally this, which was read out by a tall guy with long grey hair and a wicked grin and who said we should all listen to the Led Zeppelin song (*Stairway to Heaven*) when we got home. Maudlin? No, I really don't believe that it was:

"And as we wind on down the road
Our shadows taller than our soul.
There walks a lady we all know
Who shines white light and wants to show
How ev'rything still turns to gold.
And if you listen very hard
The tune will come to you at last.
When all are one and one is all
To be a rock and not to roll."

>

From: Steven Charteris [stevencharteris@staracademy.com]
Sent: 12/23/2012 09.16 AM GMT
To: Arthur Shilling [arthur.shilling@gammondhopes.com]
Subject: "This above all: to thine own self be true, and it must follow, as the night the day, thou canst not then be false to any man."

My dear Arthur

I can only offer words and condolences for the loss of a colleague and someone who would have been a long-lasting friend. Time is a healer and, while your loss won't diminish (and in some ways shouldn't), you will learn and grow.

I'm enormously proud of you and your achievements.

Arthur, *Richard III* was excellent. A great performance. How do I know? Because unbeknownst to you m'lad, I was there and on the first night too. You were truly excellent and I can only say that it surpassed your Mercutio. I could see a sensitive Buckingham while the anger and frustration in character (and in you) were palpable. Well done indeed. The lady next to me wanted to hand me her handkerchief and she too was shedding a tear. Very beautiful she was – red hair.

I'm delighted that Jenny Barstiff and you are good friends. Her performance in the play was sterling and she is, as you have always intimated, extremely pretty. Her tears looked real and she reminded me a touch of Mrs C in her salad days.

Professor Franklin said that indeed she did bump into you in darkest London. She recalls your essays on Eliot and Pound and said that you acquitted yourself well enough, although my recollection is somewhat different. Mind you, I do remember your essay on *La Figlia Che Piange* and that was very good – nearly put it up for the Lost Marblees and Dunnhidin Keats Poetry Award. Remember? Professor F has been enormously helpful in managing Mrs C's forthcoming court case. A law specialist should be of some help in these matters even if it is the law of jurisprudence in which Prof F specialises. Mrs C maintains that she had only meant to see if the colour of the toothbrush was the same blue as her nail polish.

Anyway, Prof F has said that she has a flat to let in North London and that I'm to tell you that it will be empty next month. It has two bedrooms and all mod cons apparently. She wonders if it would suit you, given your need to find new accommodation. I attach some photographs and the address, so do go and have a look. By the sounds of it, the terms are most reasonable. Anyway, let Prof F know your views – her number is below. You should, of course, stay in touch with your current flame-haired landlady and I'm sure that you'll be invited to her wedding.

Well, Arthur, I'd better close. Many congratulations on your promotion. See? I knew it would happen sooner or later and happen it has. Wonderful news.

Today I was approached by my publishers whom I've known for an age. They specialise in matters Shakespearian. Their new commissioning editor was in my part of the world and wanted to say hello. Over tea and muffins (my favourite as you remember) she wondered if I had any new ideas for a book. I said that I hadn't, but would think about it. And I will. She left her card. Trudy.

She said that she'd just lost her best friend. I liked her and her smile. Small world, Arthur, small world.

Best wishes, as ever… from us both. And I'll visit soon. I promise.

Steven Charteris

About the Author

SIMON MAIER has been involved in delivering events for 23 years throughout the world and for every imaginable purpose. He has also written several books on speeches, speechwriting, speechmaking, oratory and the art of communications. In the mid-1980s he led much of the event activity in the UK for the privatisation of many blue chip companies and has since been responsible for a wide variety of corporate, public and televisual events.

Simon has held a number of very senior posts with international events' agencies and communication consultancies, including his own. He is still in the industry and is passionate about great events (small as well as big) and brilliant communications. Many regard him as a great event quarterback. Despite that, he can't play American football. But he can be contacted at simonmaier@ btinternet.com.